Idiomatic Expressions and Somatic Experience in Psychoanalysis

Idiomatic Expressions and Somatic Experience in Psychoanalysis examines how verbal and non-verbal language is used in the consulting room, and how those different modes of communication interact to provide a more comprehensive picture of the patient's relational world. It is the product of a comprehensive research project exploring the affinity between idiomatic expressions and somatic behaviors and symptoms. Idiomatic expressions are viewed as bridging the gap between somatic sensations and mental experiences.

Ravit Raufman deals with one of the fundamental aspects in human life – the way our behavior is governed by unconscious primary experiences, suggesting methods with which we can decipher patient behaviors that are apparently detached and unreasonable. The first part presents case studies of people who enact and revive verbal idiomatic expressions through their behavior. The second describes how therapists use non-verbal mechanisms, operating in their own minds, to understand their patients' inner lives. Based on relational and inter-subjective approaches in psychoanalysis, the case studies illustrate the various ways in which the therapist's subjective experience is "objectively" used to learn about patients' subjective relational experience, so as to verbally formulate experiences that are pre-verbal. Raufman combines Freudian ideas regarding the affinity between somatic symptoms and verbal expressions, with a contemporary relational perspective. The book combines scientific findings with a narrative style, including life-stories of various individuals, as well as a description of the therapist's own subjective experience.

This book will appeal to clinical psychologists and psychoanalytic psychotherapists as well as anyone interested in understanding human psyche and behavior.

Ravit Raufman, Ph.D., is a clinical psychologist, group therapist and senior lecturer at the University of Haifa, Faculty of Humanity, Department of Hebrew and Comparative Literature, Israel. She also teaches at the Faculty of Education and Faculty of Social Welfare. She is Member of the Emili Sagol Creative Arts Therapies Research Center. Her research deals mostly with dreams, fairy tales, group therapy and relational psychoanalysis.

Idiomatic Expressions and Somatic Experience in Psychoanalysis

Relational and Inter-Subjective Perspectives

Ravit Raufman

Routledge
Taylor & Francis Group

LONDON AND NEW YORK

First published 2018
by Routledge
2 Park Square, Milton Park, Abingdon, Oxon OX14 4RN

and by Routledge
711 Third Avenue, New York, NY 10017

Routledge is an imprint of the Taylor & Francis Group, an informa business

© 2018 Ravit Raufman

The right of Ravit Raufman to be identified as author of this work has been asserted by her in accordance with sections 77 and 78 of the Copyright, Designs and Patents Act 1988.

All rights reserved. No part of this book may be reprinted or reproduced or utilised in any form or by any electronic, mechanical, or other means, now known or hereafter invented, including photocopying and recording, or in any information storage or retrieval system, without permission in writing from the publishers.

Trademark notice: Product or corporate names may be trademarks or registered trademarks, and are used only for identification and explanation without intent to infringe.

British Library Cataloguing-in-Publication Data
A catalogue record for this book is available from the British Library

Library of Congress Cataloging-in-Publication Data
Names: Raufman, Ravit, author.
Title: Idiomatic expressions and somatic experience in psychoanalysis : relational and inter-subjective perspectives / Ravit Raufman.
Description: New York : Routledge, 2018. | Includes bibliographical references and index.
Identifiers: LCCN 2017051555 (print) | LCCN 2018000695 (ebook) | ISBN 9781351117227 (Master) | ISBN 9781351117210 (Web PDF) | ISBN 9781351117203 (ePub) | ISBN 9781351117197 (Mobipocket/Kindle) | ISBN 9780815360988 (hardback) | ISBN 9780815361008 (pbk.)
Subjects: LCSH: Psychoanalysis. | Idioms.
Classification: LCC BF173 (ebook) | LCC BF173 .R36528 2018 (print) | DDC 150.19/5—dc23
LC record available at https://lccn.loc.gov/2017051555

ISBN: 978-0-8153-6098-8 (hbk)
ISBN: 978-0-8153-6100-8 (pbk)
ISBN: 978-1-351-11722-7 (ebk)

Typeset in Times
by Florence Production Ltd, Stoodleigh, Devon, UK

This book is dedicated to the memory of my father, Asher Golan, my mother, Ziva Golan, whose love never fades, and my beloved family: Dror, Bar, Or and Tal Raufman, who fill my life with grace.

Contents

Acknowledgements	ix
Prologue	xi

SECTION 1
From language to experience — 1

1	Below the surface	5
2	That train has left the station	19
3	What's the matter?	35
4	Digging into the past	47

SECTION 2
From experience to language — **57**

5	It does not smell good: (I smell a rat)	67
6	A dancer who does not dance	85
7	Travel far to draw near	99
8	On the record: The possibility of publicly disclosing cases of sexual abuse	111
	Index	127

Acknowledgements

My gratitude goes to the Research Authority of The University of Haifa, for supporting this project.

I am especially grateful to Charles Bath and the editorial staff at Routledge for stewarding the publication and carefully assisting with every detail.

I deeply thank Dr. Ilil Arbel, whose editing has accompanied me on my journey into the experience of language, and the language of experience. It was the pleasure of a joined enterprise that yielded this book in its final shape.

Special thanks go to the following colleagues and friends who had read parts of the manuscript in its many stages, and generously contributed their comments and suggestions: Dr. Dana Amir, Dr. Richard Billow, Dr. Robert Grossmark, Prof. Jacob Lomranz, Dr. Gila Ofer, Dr. Haim Weinberg and Dr. Yoav Yigael.

I am grateful to Bat-Chen Sneir Tenenbaum, who contributed her painting to the book's cover. The image of a ruin beautifully echoes the nature of the human psyche, and has captured my heart from the moment I saw it.

Prologue

Orly Castel-Bloom's story *Not Far from the Center of Town* opens with the protagonist, Avishai, leaving his flat remorsefully in silence, feeling that his life is a complete mess, but without even knowing why.

In this story, Dalia and Avishai's married life in the big city is depicted laconically, while Avishai, a newlywed, knows nothing about his true feelings. This story, as well as the other stories in the collection, is populated by apparently indifferent characters, who deal with their pain by continually shifting away from their real interests and desires. Consequently, they remain alien to themselves, addicted to automatic gestures and banal routines.

Regretfully, this situation is not merely fictional. The gap between the choices made by the characters in the story and their troubling distress accurately illustrates how people often become alienated from themselves. Estranged and disconnected from their inner life they often become lost, with no compass to guide them back. Many people live their lives hectically, bereft of any knowledge of their true feelings or motives. False choices are repeatedly made throughout life, causing people to fall into the same traps over and over again; impossible loves, inexplicable relationships, self-destructive habits, addictions and difficulties in family life and career are only some of the many ways people become dissociated from themselves. Sometimes, when the distress becomes unbearable, they seek therapy, also for reasons they cannot necessarily put their fingers on. This alienation is not just a matter of repression and denial, as formulated by Freud and his followers. Rather, it stems from the fact that the human psyche consists of different modes, each possessing its own language.

The human mind expresses itself in a language different from the verbal language we use in our daily lives, though these verbal and non-verbal languages share intricate relationships. Many day-to-day behaviors and symptoms may be understood in light of the relations between both languages; the more primary, sensorial and unconscious language, as well as the symbolic-verbal one.

In his book *This Craft of Verse* (2000), Borges wonders how the poet uses words employed in the ordinary, everyday commerce of life, and somehow imbues them with magic, beyond their intended purpose. However, he also notes that "words began not by being abstract, but rather by being concrete – and I suppose 'concrete' means much the same thing as 'poetic' in this case" (p. 79).

Borges asserts that the history of etymology may well demonstrate this idea: "the word 'dreary' originally meant 'blood-stained,' the word 'glad' once meant 'polished,' while the word 'threat' meant 'a threatening crowd'" (p. 79). These words that have now become abstract once had a powerful meaning, loaded with emotion and vitality.

> The word *punor* stood for thunder and for the god [of thunder]; but had we asked the men who came to England with Hengist whether the word stood for the rumbling in the sky or for the angry god, I do not think they would have been subtle enough to understand the difference. I suppose that the word carried both meanings without committing itself very closely to either one of them. I supposed that when they uttered or heard the word "thunder," they at the same time felt the low rumbling in the sky and saw the lightning and thought of the god. The words were packed with magic, they did not have a hard and fast meaning . . . poetry is not trying to take a set of logical coins and work them into magic. Rather, it is bringing language back to its original source.
>
> (p. 80)

In so suggesting, Borges focuses on the complex, ever-changing relations between the experiencing, primary language, and the verbal one, usually called "abstract."

The psychic realm from which poets draw their ability to load words with magic and emotion also governs myths, fairy tales, dreams, symbols and art. Freud called it "the unconscious," Jung named it "the collective and individual unconscious," while Lacan described it as being embedded in language. Both psychoanalytic and psychodynamic therapies focus on it. Its language is different than any other familiar language; it is a non-verbal language, in which psychic impressions are organized based on the way they are experienced. This book only touches on the part of this language's characteristics that connects it to the spoken verbal language, by using realizations of idiomatic expressions. Deciphering the words hidden behind various symptoms and identifying sensations and emotions requires an understanding of the psyche's language and its interrelations between different levels and modes. These include those which are regarded as "primary" and are mostly unconscious, governed by somatic sensations and senses, and the higher levels, which are verbal.

Although psychoanalysis has developed different approaches regarding the unconscious and the linguistic, some shared characteristics may be identified, mostly regarding the two perspectives that have considerably shaped the development of the discourse about the unconscious: the Freudian and the Jungian. Both share a common perception regarding the mental structure and identify two levels of organizing information: a *primary*, fundamental level, and a *verbal*, symbolic one. The primary, more animal-like level, is governed by drives, urges and instincts, drawing information from the senses. As time passed, various thinkers formulated different approaches to understanding the relations between the somatic and verbal layers of the mind, some of which will be presented throughout the book to exemplify the complexity of the topic and its clinical, as well as theoretical, repercussions. For those readers who are not familiar with psychoanalytic literature, I hope the book will provide an opportunity to gain a basic familiarity with the different layers and modes of the human psyche, as well as how they manifest themselves in stressful situations.

The book presents eight clinical cases in which behavioral and somatic symptoms are treated and addressed by examining and highlighting the relations between both languages.

The first part of the book, entitled "From language to experience," presents case studies in which people concretely enact and revive, through their behaviors, verbal metaphorical expressions. One such example depicts an individual who is chronically late. This behavior is understood as an unconscious re-enacting and reviving of the idiomatic expression "that train has left the station." In Hebrew, this idiom is slightly different; we say "to miss the train." This case is a chillingly accurate description reflecting a real event that had saved the patient's mother during WWII. She had escaped the concentration camps because by being late, she "missed" the train that transferred Jews to Auschwitz.

Another example is a dance teacher who constantly feels she cannot trust her own back (not to give out/to support her) while demonstrating certain exercises and movements. The case reveals a general, deep and fundamental feeling about her life – the sense that no one is "backing her up" or supporting her. This feeling turns out to be deeply rooted in her early experiences with significant others.

This part of the book deals with the unique status of idiomatic expressions in human experience, and in bridging the gap between primary-somatic experiences and the verbal metaphorical realm. Reviving and realizing these idioms on the behavioral level facilitates our understanding of the connections between concrete and symbolic modes of human experience. Deciphering the idiomatic expression hidden behind a particular behavior, symptom or dream is exemplified in this section by presenting cases in which language cloaks experience, and experience makes language apparent.

In certain situations, the experience "hidden" in language is remarkably unconscious and intricate; thus, theoretical knowledge is not enough to decipher its meaning, just as intellectual, verbal interpretations can neither reach this non-verbal experience nor touch it. This is the topic of the second part of the book, entitled "From experience to language." This section describes how therapists use the primary non-verbal mechanisms operating in their own minds, to understand something profound about their patients' inner lives. Articulately using these primary channels, therapists strive to learn about the experiences operating at the same level in their patients.

Case studies described in the book illustrate the various ways in which the therapist's subjective experience is "objectively" used to learn about patients' subjective relational experience, so as to verbally formulate experiences that are pre-verbal. In so doing, the book draws from various threads of the contemporary psychoanalytic tapestry, including mostly object relations theories, relational and intersubjective approaches.

The cases presented are not precise descriptions of real clinical situations. Due to ethical considerations, each is composed of a collage of several cases. However, they do demonstrate real issues and principles of therapeutic processes, and encounters between patients and therapists. Each contributes to the understanding of various symptoms and possible interventions.

In my ongoing attempts to find ways by which people can "speak their minds," I have found literature, and specifically, *belles-lettres*, to be a useful form for exploring the connections between conscious and unconscious processes, primary and symbolic modes. In the words of

Borges, "Life is made of poetry. Poetry is not alien – poetry is, as we shall see, lurking around the corner. It may spring on us at any moment" (2000, p. 3). In some chapters of this book I strive to touch upon the unique status of literary texts in the human psyche. Literary texts are well-suited to this task, due to their ability to describe, echo and reflect mental states, and the therapeutic value of literature has been addressed on many occasions. This is especially illustrated in the chapter "Travel far to draw near," in which a poem penned by the Hebrew poet R'ahel allows for a psychic language to unfold. The poem serves as a realm with which to create closer contact with inner experiences which cannot find their full expression in the formal language. In other cases, such as illustrated in the chapters "What's the matter?," "Below the surface" and "A dancer who does not dance," examples from fine and folk literature expand our understanding and discussion of the clinical cases presented. Sometimes, the fictional literary characters that operate on the level of poetic fiction exemplify mental states and situations. In other cases, the existence of a fictional arena, with all its complex connections to the real world of flesh and blood human beings, is significant in itself. The unique language of literary texts provides human experiences with poetic expressions not to explain or analyze, but to echo, reflect and expand the boundaries of experience. As Dana Amir has proposed, "Rather than the poet's genius for reflecting on his own existence, it is the lyrical dimension of every human being as such, which makes existence possible" (Amir, 2016, p. xiii). The human psyche cries out in an attempt to express itself and incessantly strives to minimize the gap between desires and resilient, lasting possibilities in reality.

Endeavoring to bridge the gap between the different languages of the human psyche is part of our effort to create a better connection with our inner life and adjust our daily choices to be more in step with our inner desires. At least, we can stop depriving ourselves of having a clue regarding the inevitable compromises we make in our life.

If Avishai, the protagonist of the tale *Not Far from the Center of Town*, would have known something about the reasons for his miserable life, maybe he would have acted differently, in a less alienated manner. However, for us, the readers, the opportunity to encounter this kind of detachment and estrangement in the literary arena, without clarifying or resolving it, is of therapeutic value. It creates a space in which we can establish some familiarity with a mental state in its entire – and at times contradictory – form, in a way that can penetrate our soul.

References

Amir, D. (2016). *On the Lyricism of the Mind: Psychoanalysis and Literature.* New York: Routledge.

Borges, J.M. (2000). *This Craft of Verse.* Cambridge, MA: Harvard University Press.

Castel-Bloom, O. (1987). *Not Far from the Center of Town.* Tel Aviv: Am-Oved [Hebrew].

Section I

From language to experience

LANGUAGE HIDDEN BEHIND EXPERIENCES

Idiomatic expressions that bridge the gap between somatic and mental experiences

A while ago, a patient related the following dream to me:

> I am rehearsing with an orchestra I usually play with. I'm trying to play my flute, but it is very difficult and challenging. All of a sudden, my mother comes to help me, because she realizes I'm making considerable efforts and she wants to support me. She stands next to me, on my right side.

The dreamer then explained that unlike other musical instruments, you must be careful how you hold the flute when you play with other musicians so that it won't stick in your neighbor's face.

The idiomatic expression – "to stand by me," attains a realization in the dream, by portraying a palpable picture, in which the mother stands by the dreamer's side. More specifically, she stands to her right. However, this meant the dreamer couldn't go on playing because she had no "room" to hold her flute, as her right side was now "blocked" or "taken up" by her mother. This dream narrative demonstrates in its pictorial, dreamlike language several complex, profound issues regarding how the patient's mother, although trying to help, could not give her the space she truly needed. The concrete way in which this subconscious issue came to the patient's consciousness convinced her of its relevancy, and she could finally start addressing it consciously, to understand how it influenced her inner life.

Another example is that of a young woman, who had recently become a mother. She related the following dream:

> *She goes to the sea shore. Suddenly she realizes that instead of wearing her sun hat, which protects her skin from the sun, she has on a shower cap.*

This concrete picture enabled her to discuss the different "hats" she wears in her daily life while fulfilling different roles – mother, a working woman, etc. The dream, using its unique language, conveys its messages in a very sophisticated manner. The dreamer could see – or sometimes feel – the dream messages and then work through them. In the distinctive, visual way of dreams, it managed to bypass the dreamer's defense mechanisms, allowing contact with the primary levels of the mental organization. When the patient and I discussed this dream, it was possible to talk more comprehensively about the various meanings of the dilemmas involved in becoming a mother, and of the resulting high price. Of course, she could have talked about these issues without the dream. However, the dream not only reminded her that she was preoccupied with this problem; it also demonstrated, most vividly and concretely, the deep meaning of this situation on the somatic-sensorial level, not only as an abstract idea. The dream provides a glimpse into the language of the psyche and tells us something about the psyche's way of communicating with itself.

A further example includes the very familiar and frequent idiom: "What's the point?" A young depressive patient related the following dream to me:

> *I'm standing in front of a table full of refreshments, but feel no desire for anything on the table. I think to myself: "What's the point?"*

(In Hebrew, instead of the word "point," we use the word "taste" which makes the pictorial language of the dream even more precise, as the dreamer is a Hebrew speaker). This sensorial experience is a direct translation of his mental state and also of the metaphorical meaning of the well-known idiomatic expression. It expresses the dreamer's lack of sensorial contact with his surroundings, a common characteristic of depression. The somatic senses govern the first, primary contact of a baby with his or her environment. This is how babies start becoming involved with the surrounding environment – through their first contact with the mother or other caregivers. We know that many eating disorders are also associated with the early impairment of attachment issues. The direct analogy between taste – a fundamental sense through which basic needs are satisfied – and the questions of whether life has any meaning, becomes reasonably clear in the above dream. The dream image helps us trace back and identify the origin of the depression. In a way, this example is similar to the idiom: "It doesn't smell good," which I will discuss in another chapter of this book.

As stated at the outset, the human psyche has its own unique language. The first section in the book presents therapeutic vignettes, through the adoption of theoretical frameworks with which I have been involved in recent years. It is the study of the unique status of idiomatic expressions, our ability to use words to reach non-verbal modes of experience. Identifying idiomatic expressions hidden behind a distinct symptom may function as part of the therapeutic process. This process helps to extricate the symptoms from their detached, isolated, enigmatic status, making them more accessible to consciousness. It applies in particular to what we call "somatic idioms" – idiomatic expressions that include body parts, or body gestures. These expressions have a unique status in human experience. On the somatic-sensorial/abstract continuum, they play a significant role in the way the body represents itself through language. Each of the chapters in the next section exemplifies this idea. This theoretical framework, based on early Freudian ideas, is weaved together with my relational attitude adopted in my clinical practice. I hope the book overcomes the inconsistencies in language and theory. However, I find these apparently different schools of thought to be highly associated with each other. Language is always relational. Linguistic phenomena cloaked behind various symptoms, and vice versa (sensorial and somatic reactions evoked by language), always take shape in the presence of the other, whether "internal" objects or "external" ones. Listening to the ways primary processes can be allowed to unfold in language, and using the intersubjective matrix and our own relational world to validate, or provide various symptoms with meanings, may be the venue in which these different theoretical orientations meet. Drawing on Bion's assertion that interpretations are only useful if they share the qualities of passion, sense and myth, Cartwright takes this to mean that "containing interpretations work on linking sensory information outside the dreaming process (the 'proper object'), with myth (coherent products of the 'dream object': the dreamed up idea of a precious symbiosis) in the context of shared emotions" (Cartwright, 2013, p. 98). This way, he emphasizes the intersubjective component in the theory of thinking, in which the containing quality of the mother, as well as the therapist, plays central role. Other analysts also addressed the relational variations of Bion's theory of thinking (see Billow, 2003). In this book I alternate between concepts and ideas coined and developed by different schools of thought in psychoanalysis, in the hope that this will not confuse the readers, but rather expand the ways we understand each of them.

References

Billow, R. (2003). Relational Variations of the "Container-Contained," *Contemporary Psychoanalysis*, 39(1): 27–50.

Cartwright, D. (2013). Clinical Features of the Container Function, *Psychoanalytic Psychotherapy in South Africa*, 21(2): 73–104.

Chapter 1

Below the surface

> It was so beautiful and so fine, the likes of which could never have been woven in the world above.
> (From the fairy tale *The Three Feathers*)

Dreams open a concealed door into a place where new, fascinating modes of conversation are permitted between my patients and me. From this space, we set out on a shared journey, a quest for meanings and function. The first chapter of this book, therefore, discusses this intriguing subject and presents one of the several possible techniques of working with dreams – communicating the realization of the idiomatic expression, which so often characterizes the unique language of dreams and fairy tales. These are the two main topics of my academic and clinical occupations.

Many developments have occurred in psychoanalytic thought since the age of Freud. However, despite the many resulting changes in the status of dreams and how we use them in the therapeutic endeavor, they continue to engage the various psychoanalytic approaches. The dream's unique language, which often invites primary, sensual, and visual scenes, improves the contact with multifaceted layers of the human psyche. Deciphering an idiomatic expression hidden behind a concrete event in the dream helps to touch upon the dream's location on the border between the somatic and metaphorical aspects of the human psyche.

In the case I am describing in this chapter, Rebecca, a woman in her fifties, was dreaming that she was resting with her husband on their double bed.

Strangely, the bed's location was not apparent; it was not in the usual place in the bedroom. Under the bed something was stirring, perhaps the sea or some troubled waters. Suddenly, a childhood friend appeared, and the scene shifted to another time and location. Rebecca woke up, feeling baffled and uncomfortable. She said she was familiar with this vague malaise since it had accompanied her for years, but seemed detached from her current waking life. Insisting that this sensation was unrelated to her pleasant and comfortable waking life, Rebecca nevertheless felt it was important enough to begin therapy.

What I was called to address was the gap between the image of the couple resting comfortably on their bed, above the surface, and Rebecca's discomfort, caused by the strange stirring under the bed, below the surface. We are often disturbed by unknown causes, having lost contact with our own inner life. Many people describe their situation as apparently "having it all," but they do not feel free and happy. Sometimes they even suffer from severe stress that seems unrelated to their situation. This gap reminds us that the human psyche has its own, often vague and enigmatic language. An important role of the psychotherapeutic endeavor is to build bridges that enable us to "speak" our mind and decipher this language. Such understanding allows us to examine our therapeutic methods and to reach the deeper layers of human experience. It helps us to find the words needed to access the non-verbal areas of our primary experiences. The psyche's non-verbal language termed by Freud the "Primary Process," often uses symbols and images.

Since typically a bed is located in the bedroom, the ambivalence of Rebecca's dream bed's location is disconnected and detached from its usual context in reality and moved to a different sphere, while under the bed lurks the turbulent sea, or just "something" in the dream's language. This scene depicts the dreamer's situation in life. If we look at it as if it were a picture, we can see how it visually represents the image of a mental state. The dream image reveals that "something is troubling the dreamer," and shows exactly where this "something" is located – under the bed, below the surface of Rebecca's apparently relaxed relations with her husband. When we examine the possible meaning of the dream, it is necessary to discuss its idioms as part of the unique language of the psyche, translating images into words.

Freud studied the relationships between verbal expressions and somatic symptoms during the early stages of the development of his psychoanalytic theory. In *Studies on Hysteria*, Breuer and Freud described the creation of somatic symptoms as a symbolization of verbal expressions (Breuer and Freud, 1895). Yigael attempts to follow the development of Freud's idea, referring to the case of Cecily Koertner (2001, pp. 179–180). In this case, Freud described how in one of Cecily's acute attacks of facial neuralgia, she remembered a time of being furious with her husband. These bitter feelings followed a conversation during which he had insulted her. Suddenly she put her hand on her cheek and cried out loudly, apparently in great pain, saying: "It was like a slap in the face." The somatic pain was indicative of a particular kind of psychic suffering.

We can explain the creation of symbolic conversion by the simultaneous presence of thoughts accompanied by both physical and somatic pain. The latter represents the former through what Freud calls the "Associative reverberation of the psychic life" (Bruer and Freud, 1895, p. 252).

In another example, Cecily told Freud that when she was fifteen years old, she was lying in bed under the strict supervision of her grandmother. She felt a sharp pain between her eyes. Freud's analysis explained that the pain was associated with her grandmother's "penetrating" stare and the belief that her grandmother suspected her of something. The unpleasant feeling of being "under the scrutinizing eye" of someone, with suspicion directed against her, was converted into somatic pain.

Yigael mentions that Freud's use of the "symbolic" concept is different, almost antithetical to its conventional use, even his own later use (2001, p. 179). For example, when we relate to a flag as a symbol, the effect is a high concentration of values, standpoints and emotions in one object (the extent of which cannot be accurately assessed). In Freud's later works, the somatic symptom becomes a representative symbol that implies or stands for an abstract idea or repressed conflict. Conversely, while working on *Studies on Hysteria*, and within the context of the affiliation between verbal expression and somatic expression, Freud argued that the symptom is a precise translation of an idiom into a distinct sensation. Freud even adds that this is not a matter of an overdeveloped imagination; the hysteric simply relates literally to the linguistic expression. After many insulting remarks, the feeling of "a stab in the heart" or "a slap in the face" revives a sensation to which the linguistic expression owes its origin (Bruer and Freud, 1895, p. 254). It appears that Freud is saying that we are speaking of the simplest and most primitive verbal expressions, connected to sensation in an automatic manner, similar to the connection between sensations and the body's various parts. The hysteric is "right" in preserving the original meaning of words, and indicates the outstanding strength of their innervation.

While developing psychoanalysis, Freud attributed great importance to various aspects of relating to language. However, the attempt to view the symptom as an exact equivalent of a verbal expression was almost entirely neglected, at the price of seeing the symptom as a symbolic expression of an unconscious conflict. During the period of *Studies on Hysteria*, Freud didn't connect the symptoms to early childhood experiences – a connection which we now view as essential to understanding the shared origin of early sensor-somatic experiences and idiomatic expressions involving body parts. Many other analytic researchers have tried to follow Freud's ideas regarding the affinity between symptoms and language, including Klein, Winnicott, Bion, Ogden, Bick, McDougall, Meltzer, Tustin, Lacan and others. However, none of these analysts specifically discussed the unique status of somatic idioms, its distinction from other verbal expressions and how they are transformed into somatic symptoms.

Even McDougall, who relates to verbal expressions that have a direct connection to physiological phenomena, and argues (similarly to Ogden, Bick and others) that the symptoms originate in pre-verbal experiences (McDougall, 1989), offers a theoretical mechanism which is somewhat different from the clinical one. Furthermore, she fails to explain the connection between verbal expression and myocardial infarction satisfactorily. And yet, her ideas are in line with many other analytical attempts to place the earliest impressions of life outside the symbolic/linguistic zone. These conceptualizations show a clear awareness of possible connections between somatic experiences and verbal expressions but still view the earliest somatic area as being pre-verbal.

Clinical psychology regards words and verbal expressions as having the power to reach the deepest levels of the body/mind, which is one of the leading principles that psychoanalytic therapy strives to achieve. At the same time, the psychoanalytic theory assumes that there are layers within the mental systems that are pre-verbal. Therefore, the theory ought to explain precisely how the verbal can and should approach and reach this pre-verbal layer, which is said by the same theory to exist beyond its grasp. In this book, I demonstrate how exposing the relations between the somatic level of mental organization and verbal aspects in human experience might, in some situations, be of therapeutic value, since it creates a type of bridge. This bridge serves to connect primary and secondary thought processes, as well as somatic symptoms and verbal idiomatic expressions. Therefore, idioms and their realizations in the forms of behavioral symptoms might serve as a fundamental key to investigating these different layers. As exemplified in the cases described in this book, idiomatic expressions exist on the border between sensations emerging from somatic experiences and the verbal realm.

Let's return to Rebecca's dream. It provided her with a visual way of observing her life and seeing "with her own eyes" that something was stirring below the surface. It is worth noting that in many languages, *seeing* means *understanding*. When we say "*I see what you mean*" we are saying that we understand. Connecting seeing with understanding is so deeply ingrained that it reveals how our somatic senses and sensations are interwoven with higher functions. Psychoanalysis uses the word *insight* to describe a profound emotional knowing. Through the dream, the dreamer came to understand, or indeed see something vital, which was previously hidden, about her mental state and about the issues that are troubling her. This knowledge penetrated and percolated beyond the verbal realm, paving its path deep inside the psyche and below the surface where troubled waters flowed.

How can we tell whether or not our elucidation is worthwhile? Is there, in fact, a "true" interpretation of a dream? A partial answer to this question may emerge from the dreamer's responses, as the dreamer either owns or denies the knowledge. When patients tell me their dreams, I check whether my interpretation has somehow touched and moved them. Does it mean something to them? Does it echo and resonate, strike a chord? If not, it is still possible to work with my misinterpretation and see what it evokes? If it does ring true, we can continue along this path and pursue the matter on a deeper level. It soon became apparent that Rebecca was deeply moved by my suggestion that turbulent water swirled below her apparently comfortable relations with her husband. The next step was to find out what was the actual disturbance below the surface.

In human experience, the idiom "below the surface" is heavily loaded. Freud was well aware of it while formulating his topographic model regarding different layers of consciousness (the unconscious, preconscious and conscious), comparing them to a layered geological mass in which the deepest one is the unconscious.

I use fairy tales to examine the idiom's many underlying meanings. Fairy tales exist outside the psychoanalytic field but have been perceived as a valuable source of knowledge since the age of Freud. Freud's interest in folklore and fairy tales was not a marginal branch of his theory. He maintained that psychoanalysis recognized the vital role fairy tales played in our mental life and that in some cultures the act of recollecting fairy tales played a role equivalent to that of recollecting childhood memories (Freud, 1913).

Other analytic scholars subsequently adopted this view. From a Freudian perspective, the work of Bettelheim (1976) was highly popular. From a Jungian perspective, Neumann (1976) and Marie-Louis von Franz (1978) viewed fairy tales as encompassing significant information about the unconscious. Various folkloristic interpretations also applied psychoanalytic perspectives, such as Dundes (1978), Barzilai (1990) and Raufman (2009) among others; all of whom identified fairy tales as an essential subject of investigation. Some of the central concepts in psychoanalysis are taken from folklore, including the Oedipus complex, the panic phenomenon, narcissism, Eros and Thanatos.

Freud claimed that understanding symbols in dreams required familiarity with their appearance in folklore. The wide distribution of fairy tales, their prevalence in different cultural regions, and the repetitive themes and motifs they presented over the generations, testify to their relevancy, which goes beyond a particular individual or society. The fact that the same narratives were told over and over again in different eras may validate the idea of universal and shared characteristics in human thought, in which fantasy plays a central role. Marie Louise von Franz, the Jungian psychoanalyst, regarded fairy tales as the purest and most direct expression of mental processes and considered their examination as more valuable than any other material.

In previous works, Yoav Yigael and I reversed this approach. Instead of psychoanalyzing fairy tales by using existing analytic models, we used fairy tales as a source of knowledge of the human psyche. We examined the validation of existing models and formulated new conceptualizations, attempting to trace the language of the infantile psyche or, in other words, to determine the primary levels of mental organization (Raufman and Yigael, 2014, Raufman and Yigael, in press; Yigael and Raufman, 2016). Following this, I suggest that like dreams, fairy tales echo the language of the primary psyche. It is therefore not surprising that they continue to be told in so many different cultures around the world. Favorite tales such as Snow White, Cinderella and Sleeping Beauty are narrated in numerous variations in so many distant and remote regions, that one can't help but ask the question: What is it about these tales that has captured the minds and hearts of so many people? Also, similar to the language of dreams, the fairy tale genre is located along the seam line between thinking in words and "thinking" in images.

Before returning to Rebecca's dream, let's examine the idiom "below the surface," as it appears in a well-known fairy tale named *The Three Feathers*. It begins with an aging king who must decide to which of his three sons he should bequeath his kingdom. On three separate occasions, the king asks the young men to bring him valuable articles – the most beautiful carpet, the finest ring and the loveliest woman. On each quest, they blow a feather into the air and follow it in search of the desired object. The eldest son's feather flies east, the second son's feather flies west, but the youngest son (called "the Simpleton") sees that his feather falls straight to the ground after going only a short distance. The older brothers laugh at the Simpleton who has to stand there where the feather has fallen. At first, the Simpleton is sad, but then he notices a trap-door by his feather. Lifting the trap-door, he sees a stairway; it leads him into the underground Toads' Kingdom, from which he brings the finest treasures and wins the crown.

The above description is a short synopsis of the well-known tale, which appears in many versions around the world and has attained various psychoanalytic interpretations. The story exemplifies the relations between the pictorial and verbal modes of experience. Like Rebecca's dream of resting with her husband above troubled waters, *The Three Feathers* dictates that meaningful possessions rest below the surface. Adopting a Freudian perspective, Bettelheim suggested interpreting the story using Freud's topographic model to reveal the different levels of consciousness, and that art emerges from the unconscious (Bettelheim, 1976). However, I believe he missed a salient poetic feature of the fairy tale genre, existing not on the content level, but rather on the form. The fairy tale illustrates the different levels of the psyche not only through content but by realizing an idiomatic expression common in the daily use of language. Bettelheim did not address the existence of realizations of idioms. The fairy tale does not present this as a symbolic or metaphoric idea. It is actually and pictorially shown in the story's overt plot; the son must physically go deep below the surface of the earth to retrieve the coveted treasures. The tale portrays a visual picture of an abstract idea relating to the idiomatic expression "below the surface." This is the fairy tale's unique language and its way of showing that on the surface something is insufficient, and he who remains on the surface without delving deep below it can never become a king, i.e., can never become the master of his own life. Like Rebecca's dream, the meaningful part of the tale is not necessarily in its content. Instead, it is the graphic way in which it renders its messages, clearly and directly observed, like a movie. This non-verbal mode of expression, similar to dream language, allows for the transmission of messages that can touch and echo the most primary levels of the psyche. Then, it enables the dreamer, or the tale's listeners, to undergo a transformative experience. We can say, that the dream's meaning rests "below the surface."

The fairy tale may play a significant role in helping to understand how verbal language connects to primary, non-verbal aspects of human experience. The apparently magical, fantastic elements appearing in the plots are a precise translation of ordinary, even banal idiomatic expressions describing fundamental aspects of human experience. As one of the initial attempts to portray human experience in prose, the fairy tale may be regarded as a "living fossil" (a way of life that did not change for prolonged time periods in evolutionary terms), while other forms of narrative became obsolete or had undergone a metamorphosis. It preserves ancient modes of human thought and as such it teaches us about other living fossils that have been retained in our psyche's individual and community levels for generations.[1]

Encoding an idiomatic expression behind a concrete plot detail helps interweave the thread connecting these different modes of thinking. The fairy tale does not tell us that something is happening below the surface; it shows us a picture. Similarly, Rebecca's dream did not tell us about, but instead showed us the troubled waters, swirling below the surface. Idiomatic expressions may also be encoded behind various behaviors and symptoms, some of which may be quite bizarre, relentless and apparently meaningless – much like the fairy tales' seemingly magical and strange plots. In this regard we may recall Freud's original suggestion to view the symptom as communication. Even though this idea seems obvious, it has become lost in recent years.

Many people are familiar with the feeling of not understanding themselves. It is not uncommon for even educated, intelligent and well-functioning people to find themselves governed by apparently unreasonable symptoms. In the second part of the dream, Rebecca saw a childhood friend who she associated with an earlier period of her life. At that time, Rebecca was tormented by the indecision of whether or not to marry her present husband. The friend, who seemed to "just pass through" the dream, visually bridged the troubled waters of the earlier period of trepidation regarding the life-changing dilemma of her prospective marriage.

The dream's pictorial language invited Rebecca to visually observe the affinity between what troubled her in the present and the concerns of the past, both involving her relationship with her husband. It reminded her that even if she believed that the dilemma had long been resolved, she must not ignore the association between past doubts and present discomfort. She had to address the repression and denial and deal with the suppressed core problems by hauling them from below the surface into the light.

I doubt this transformation in consciousness would have been possible through intervention that remained only on the verbal level. Like the older sons in the fairy tale *The Three Feathers*, any quest for meaning that remains "on the surface" would not bring treasures. The visual images were essential, and their revelations allowed Rebecca to connect with the more primary levels of the psyche, where she could acquire in-depth knowledge. The dream's language, located on the border between modes of thinking and experience, and the realization that this language is also evident in fairy tales, paved the path to a new realm that entered into the arena of our therapeutic enterprise and served as an agent of change.

Another example of this phenomenon was experienced by a patient named Rachel. She studied physical education, but could not use her own back in the exercises she gave to other women. She would repeatedly say that "no one backs her up." While she related to the metaphoric meaning of this idiom, meaning that her parents did not support her financially or emotionally and that she had no intimate partner for several years, she also experienced this "lack of backing," or support, in a physical, concrete manner.

Rachel repeated this statement so often that it made me think I needed to examine the possible origin of the expression more closely. In Hebrew, her native language, the phrase means: "I have no back." What experience could have engendered such a strange thought? How could one have "no back?"

Highly engaged in physical exercise and extremely aware of her body, Rachel said she had a strong back, but when she worked out with other women, she always made them do back exercises but never did them herself. After thinking about it for a while, she commented: "Babies, in their first few weeks of life, need someone to support their backs; they cannot hold themselves upright alone." Few interactions are so simple, yet so beautiful, as the feeling of somebody holding you and gently supporting your back.[2]

This association relates to the act of the parents supporting the baby's back, one of the most primary and meaningful experiences in every child–parent relationship. It contributes to the feeling that one is not alone, that someone is helping you to "hold on" in an extremely concrete manner. Over the years, however, the meaning of the word "support" becomes symbolic. Idiomatic expressions, such as "nobody backs me up," do not necessarily relate to the actual physical support of the physical back, but rather indicate the painful adjustment from the stage in which a supportive caretaker who was once there, holding us, is now gone. The way parents support the baby's back could be the possible origin of the expression "back me up," since there is a point in life when the individual no longer needs to be physically supported by another but is expected to function independently. Feelings of longing for this lost early stage of support are replaced by other things and people that fulfill and "support" the individual. We should remember that the use of the word "holding" in psychoanalysis is also symbolic, relating to a mental, psychological holding. Winnicott, who was the first to coin this term, associated it with the early stage of development in which "holding" was a concrete physical act, performed by the mother, who was equipped with what he called "primary maternal preoccupation" (Winnicott, 1985).

Similar to the fairy tale's function as a living fossil, many persistent and bizarre behaviors and symptoms may be a precise translation of ordinary and banal idiomatic expressions. The experiences behind them, however, are quite deep and meaningful. To gain a deeper understanding, we need to consider the relations between concrete and symbolic layers of human experiences, and the way they were perceived by several psychoanalytic approaches.

It is a common assumption that during the first experiences of life a baby cannot differentiate itself from the environment. The process of differentiation between me/not me, between fantasy and reality, is called *symbolization* and is considered the most central and essential process of mental life. Language plays a significant role in this process, as it creates a mediating space between subject and object. Language provides names and places for the components of the self (sensations, feelings and thoughts) as well as for external objects (mother, father), and allows for substituting words for things. It is the central medium used to identify, dismantle and combine mental material, enabling the individual to recognize and differentiate between the internal and the external.

The process also requires the ability to play with the components of me/not me and is the function of the *transitional object*. In Winnicott's terms, it is used to bridge and mediate between external objects that are perceived by the senses, and the internal objects which are not perceived by the senses and have no corporeal reality. Melanie Klein identified two levels in the development of symbolic thinking (see Segal, 2002). In the first, identified with the schizo-paranoid predisposition, part of the self is identified with the object. In the second, identified with the depressive predisposition, the symbol stands for the object.

The examples presented in this book, including Rebecca's dream and Rachel's symptom, demonstrate that it is possible to identify the existence of a verbal level imprinted in earlier physical experiences, that language can partially describe the earliest, remotest experiences, and that their expressions are part of our daily existence. Thomas Ogden depicts a third mode of experience, more primitive than the two described by Klein

(Ogden, 1989). It is termed the "autistic-contiguous position" and is understood as a sensory-dominated, pre-symbolic area of experience in which the most primitive form of meaning is generated. Based on the organization of sensory impressions, particularly on the skin's surface, its pre-symbolic nature makes it extremely difficult to capture in words. Ogden suggests that when the maternal caretaking functions, such as holding and supporting the baby, are carried out correctly, the infant's needs are satisfied, leading to proper development. Under these conditions, a sensorial ground is enabled – a primary sense of physical and emotional vitality.

Among other thinkers, Ogden assumes that the primary processes which he calls *the primitive edge of experience*, consist of experiences which are so early and primary, that they take place outside of the linguistic realm. However, he may have missed some noteworthy observations regarding the affinity between language and body, as evident in the examples he presents to validate his theory. Specifically, he did not relate to the unique status of idiomatic expressions and their realizations in various symptoms, behaviors and situations. In his description of the therapy of Mrs. L., for example, a woman who suffered from severe anxiety and diffuse tension, Ogden explained that the only way she found temporary relief was to cut herself with a razor all over her body (Ogden, 1989, p. 34). After the patient had shared that she had felt as if she were coming apart at the seams, Ogden reports:

> I said that I thought she was feeling as if she was coming apart in the most literal way, and that she felt as if her skin were already lacerated in the way she had imagined lacerating herself. It was late in the afternoon and getting cold in the office. I said, "It's cold in here," and got up to turn on the heater. She said, "It is," and seemed to calm down soon after that. She said that for reasons that she did not understand, she had been extremely "touched" by my saying that it was cold and by turning the heater on; it was such an ordinary thing to say and do. I believe that my putting the heater on acknowledged a shared experience of the growing coldness in the air and contributed to the creation of a sensory surface between us. I was using my own feelings and sensations in a largely unconscious "ordinary" way . . . which felt to the patient as if I had physically touched her and held her together. The sensory surface mutually created in that way was the opposite of the experience of "coming apart at the seams," it facilitated a mending of her psychological-sensory surface which felt as if it had been shredded in the course of the patient's interaction with her mother.

This sensory "holding" (Winnicott 1960a) dimension of the analytic relationship and setting operated in conjunction with the binding power of symbolic interpretation (formulated on the basis of the intersubjectivity of the transference-countertransference).

(Ogden, 1989, p. 35)

This brilliant example taken from Ogden's practice demonstrates how the realization of idiomatic expressions may bridge the gap between different modes of experience. However, he seems to miss the most powerful component regarding his intervention: the double meaning of the word "touched," which is simultaneously concrete and metaphoric. When his patient admitted she was "touched," she was combining both aspects of experience – sensing the touch on the surface of her skin in the literal sense, as the room's temperature became more suitable to that of her body, and sharing her gratitude for the symbolic meanings inherent in this gesture. The same applies for other realizations of somatic idioms hidden behind Ogden's "ordinary act" – the feeling that their relations felt "cold," and became warmer after he turned on the heater. It is reasonable to assume that Ogden was aware of this. However, he did not focus his ideas on the particular status of somatic idioms and their location on the border between the somatic and metaphoric, nor did he mention the idea that language, in the first place, is ingrained in somatic experiences.

In our shared project, Yoav Yigael and I suggested that parts of the primary experiences are already structured in language; idiomatic expressions exemplify this idea in both a metaphoric and concrete manner (Raufman and Yigael, 2011). This idea brings us back to Freud's perspective regarding the affinity between somatic symptoms and verbal idiomatic expression, as presented in the case study of Cecily. We are called upon to re-examine this idea in the clinic, in light of the theoretical developments made since the early days of Freud. Apart from the developments made in the study of metaphors, the unique status of the idiomatic expression and its location on the border between the somatic and metaphoric realm has yet to receive its deserved attention. This is one of the challenges of this book. The idea that early somatic experiences are already embedded in language is not an easy task to prove; after all, we are exploring apparently non-verbal experiences. The examples presented here and in coming chapters demonstrate how language is embedded within a somatic experience or, more precisely, a specific linguistic element, the idiomatic expression.

We should remember that language is formed out of somatic experiences and has some of its origins in the nervous system. We are discussing experiences whose verbal expressions, meant to represent them, are already embedded in the experience itself. It is possible that these idiomatic expressions emerge from somatic experiences. Even if a causative relationship cannot be proved, the affinity between the somatic and verbal aspects can be detected. In her dream, Rebecca could not identify the source of her discomfort and therefore found it difficult to relate to her sense of unease and find future remedies. Similarly to Avishai, the protagonist in the story *Not Far from the Center of Town*, (mentioned in the prologue) she felt detached from her inner motives. She knew how to speak about her life in general, even to provide many details, but she did not feel emotionally connected to this information. Once the positive trajectory shift in our therapeutic discourse occurred, following the pictorial image appearing in her dream, a deep, emotional connection with her experiences became possible. Before this breakthrough, she had not dared to open this subject, not even with herself. Gradually she was able to express it in therapy, and later, to discuss it with her husband, in a way that facilitated their communication and opened up a new space in which to better cope with their daily life.

Notes

1 For further reading regarding the ways fairy tales function as living fossils, and the phenomenon of realization of idiomatic expressions in fairy tales, see Raufman and Weinberg, 2017.
2 This case study, as well as some other ideas presented in this chapter, were also discussed in two previous works authored together with Yoav Yigael. See Raufman, R. and Yigael, Y. (2010). "Feeling Good in Your Own Skin," Part I: Primary Levels of Mental Organization, *American Journal of Psychoanalysis*, 70: 361–385; Raufman, R. and Yigael, Y. (2011). "Feeling Good in Your Own Skin," Part II: Idiomatic Expressions: The Language's Way to Connect with the Primary Levels of Mental Organization, *American Journal of Psychoanalysis*, 71: 16–36.

References

Barzilai, S. (1990). Reading "Snow White": The Mother's Story, *Signs: Journal of Women in Culture and Society*, 15(3): 515–534.
Bettelheim, B. (1976). *The Use of Enchantments: The Meaning and Importance of Fairy Tales*. New York: Knopf.
Breuer, J. and Freud, S. (1985). Studies on Hysteria. In: J. Strachey (Ed. and Trans.) (1962), *The Standard Edition of the Complete Psychological Works of Sigmund Freud, Vol. 2*. London: Hogarth Press.

Dundes, A. (1978). To Love My Father All: A Psychoanalytic Study of the Folktale Source of King Lear. In: *Essays in Folkloristic*. Bloomington, IN: Folklore Institute, pp. 207–222.
Freud, S. (1913). The Occurrence in Dreams of Material from Fairy Tales. In: J. Strachey (Ed. and Trans.) (1953–74), *The Standard Edition of the Complete Psychological Works of Sigmund Freud, Vol. 12*. London: Hogarth Press.
McDougall, J. (1989). *Theatres of the Body: A Psychoanalytic Approach to Psychosomatic Illness*. New York: Norton.
Neumann, E. (1976). *Amor and Psyche: The Psychic Development of the Feminine*. R. Manheim (Ed. and Trans.). Princeton, NJ: Princeton University Press.
Ogden, T.H. (1989). *The Primitive Edge of Experience*. London: J. Aronson.
Raufman, R. (2009). The Birth of Fingerling as a Feminine Protection, *Western Folklore*, 68(1): 49–71.
Raufman, R. and Weinberg, H. (2017). *Fairy Tales and the Social Unconscious: The Hidden Language*. London: Karnac.
Raufman, R. and Yigael, Y. (2010), "Feeling Good in Your Own Skin," Part I: Primary Levels of Mental Organization, *American Journal of Psychoanalysis*, 70, pp. 361–385.
Raufman, R. and Yigael, Y. (2011). "Feeling Good in Your Own Skin," Part II: Idiomatic Expressions: The Language's Way to Connect with the Primary Levels of Mental Organization, *American Journal of Psychoanalysis*, 71: 16–36.
Raufman, R. and Yigael, Y. (2014). Little Red Riding Hood and the Fragmentation of Parent–Child Structure, *Academic Research Journal of Psychology and Counseling*, 1(4): 31–41.
Raufman, R. and Yigael, Y. (in press). The Primary Psyche from the Wonder-Tales' Point of View, *American Journal of Psychoanalysis*.
Segal, H. (2002). *Introduction to the Work of Melanie Klein*. London: Karnac.
von Franz, M.L. (1978). *An Introduction to the Psychology of Fairy Tales*. Irving, TX: Spring Publication.
Winnicott, D.W. (1985). Primary Maternal Preoccupation. In: *Collected Papers*. New York: Basic Books, pp. 300–305.
Yigael, Y. (2001). Dual Identification and the "Weight of Responsibility", *Psychoanalysis and Contemporary Thought*, 24(2): 175–202.
Yigael, Y. and Raufman, R. (2016). *Fairy Tales and the Impressive Language of Human's Psyche*. Tel Aviv: Resling [Hebrew].

Chapter 2

That train has left the station

Danny, my brand new patient, arrived late to our very first meeting. As I sat alone in my clinic, waiting for him to come, I wondered about the underlying reason for his tardiness. Did I offer clear directions? Did he encounter other difficulties? Was this a chronic symptom of his? Staring at the empty couch, I felt anticipation for something whose quality became apparent to me only in retrospect.

Ten minutes had passed before a tall, handsome, lively and vigorous man walked into my office. Danny is a happily married father of a son and a daughter, and he holds a high position in an engineering company. His wife referred him to therapy, complaining that "he is chronically late." His high position at work allowed him scheduling flexibility, but it did not prevent him from showing up late to important meetings and conference calls, impeding his success. This behavior also took a toll on his family life. Events, celebrations and weekend activities were always delayed, leaving family and friends frustrated and disappointed. Within Danny's fairly good life, the pattern of tardiness has been conducted like an enigmatic, isolated capsule; a secret code that had to be solved.

Obviously, Danny is not the only person in the world who maintains unhealthy patterns that contradict his standards and jeopardize his ability to function in various areas of life. He represents one of many examples of the unique language of the human psyche and its layers – the verbal, more conscious layer, often regarded as "reason," and the more primary unconscious layer, often manifesting itself through apparently bizarre, maladaptive behaviors. The possible meaning conveyed by these seemingly strange, detached symptoms is a major question with which we have been engaged in therapy, and which has also preoccupied Danny in his own life. What could a symptom such as perpetual tardiness tell us about an issue that cannot be otherwise resolved?

Chronic lateness is a common phenomenon. Various interpretations in psychological literature were proposed throughout the years to address it, including issues of domination, the struggle between forces and even manifestations of attitudes toward death. Alongside these general propositions, our challenge was to learn more about the secret language of Danny's symptom and its unique, private and idiosyncratic meaning. I felt that there was no need to provide Danny with practical coaching and techniques regarding time management. Danny seemed to be a high-functioning person, well organized in the other aspects of his life. He thoroughly recognized what was good and what was not and did not seek behavioral therapy or coaching. Rather, he needed to understand his mysterious language, probably like deciphering cryptographs; something that would foster a different kind of talk and invite non-verbal, primary layers to take part in the conversation. We set on a shared journey, with tardiness remaining an ongoing issue in both our therapy and Danny's life.

In one of our sessions, I asked Danny to tell me about his family. He had two younger sisters, and his parents owned a small stationery shop. It seems they did pretty well. I also asked him to tell me more about the family history during WWII. Much of his parents' past was shrouded in mystery, but he was aware that they came from Eastern Europe after losing all their relatives in the war. His parents were determined to immigrate to Israel and establish a new home and family out of the ruins, hoping to create a brighter future and give their children a fresh start, free of the despair that often characterized families of Holocaust survivors. Danny's mother imparted that the Nazis put all of her relatives, without exception, on the trains, though she never revealed their exact destination. However, out of his general knowledge regarding the war, Danny put the pieces together and completed the picture for himself.

Since his early childhood, the word "trains" was loaded with confusion for Danny. In his kindergarten, the children used to play with toy trains and sing the lovely children's song about the train ride in the mountain. This beautiful image never harmonized with the way his mother pronounced the very same word. Out of her mouth, it sounded like a wild, ancient animal. As a young child, his mother was saved from the Nazis by a Christian woman who hid her in her house, and her rescue has always been perceived as an unexplained miracle. Apart from that, the war was never a topic of discussion and Danny used to describe his parents as "happy and vigorous."

For several months, the direction of the therapy remained ambiguous and unclear. Danny recounted daily life details over and over again. He was long-winded about events and activities, but words seemed to have no meanings. His tardiness kept preoccupying us, but any interpretation remained ineffective. There were moments, pregnant with embarrassment, in which we were staring at each other, gazing into space, bothered by the silence prevailing between us and wondering about the gap between the affection we felt toward each other and the difficulty of being together, sharing the same room. Only in retrospect did I realize that those were moments of incubation, a time in which we deprived ourselves of words so that a new experience could emerge; something that was yet to undergo mentallization.

Neither of us wanted to ruin the seemingly harmonious atmosphere, but avoiding contact with fearful experiences that had the potential to destroy it left us unable to touch each other. Something felt sparse, partial, missing. Intellectually, I knew that this situation was part of Danny's relational world, having been raised in a family that was not allowed to feel sorrow and was compelled to happiness no matter what. However, I was not yet sure what was my part in the scene, especially concerning how I felt about his repeated tardiness. I did not feel angry, forgotten or unimportant; on the contrary, I liked Danny and was happy with his presence in my life. It was, rather, a sense of worry that was only relieved when he arrived, but time and time again we could only have a pleasant but meaningless meeting.

In the egalitarian spirit of relational approaches, I considered sharing my feelings with Danny about what I suspected was happening between us, but I could not bring myself to do it, as it felt too intrusive. Here, I harness theory to justify this choice, and concur with Grossmark who emphasizes *the unobtrusive relational analyst* (Grossmark, 2012). Grossmark foregrounds "the analyst's receptivity to patient's experiences of deadness, nonexistence, being in bits, or difficulties in simply going on being." He suggests that:

> The experience of states such as these can be interrupted by an analyst's focus on the verbal realm as expressed, for example, by curiosity and the analyzing of what the patient is doing and/or eliciting in others and in the analyst.
>
> (p. 631)

In such situations Grossmark prefers silence, quietness, patience and not speaking about the countertransference, reminding us that these should not be conflated with neutrality or one-person psychology, and that silence is not a synonym for "no words." Rather, in certain regressive states, silence can be part of a co-constructed experience and a way of being with the patient.

Grossmark takes these concepts from Balint (1968), who had formulated the idea of "benign regression," as well as from Reis (2009) who suggests enactive witnessing and privileging the silent accompanying of the therapist when painful traumatic enactments take place in the treatment, and Slochower (1996; 2004) who emphasizes that the analyst can utilize a "holding" position when "intersubjective exploration can be disruptive rather than facilitative" (Slochower, 1996, p. 34, in Grossmark, 2012, p. 633).

I used these helpful references, as well as Grossmark's notable clinical illustration, to further think about Danny's therapy. I would add, parenthetically, that working on the countertransference could rarely, if ever, be done alone. In addition to peer-supervision, the therapists' own treatment and so forth, reading the ideas mentioned above does not only expand our knowledge. It helps us bear and tolerate regressive states in which our being with our patients cannot be taken for granted; states in which we have to allow ourselves to be in the dark for a while.

Returning to Danny

The positive trajectory shift occurred when Danny shared a dream he had the night before our session. He could not recall the exact details, except for one image he remembered vividly and which left a significant mark. He was standing in the middle of a tumultuous junction in an unknown place, where trains rapidly and noisily crossed each other. Similarly to his childhood memories, the trains in the dream took the shape of wild, ancient animals, although they lacked tails or ears. They loped forward like predators, heading in the direction of an unknown destination.

Like other subjects raised throughout our therapy, Danny experienced this dream as estranged and detached, as if it belonged to someone else. For me, however, it was the first time I felt relieved. The apparently bizarre images of "predatorial trains" made sense to me more than all the other correct words overused by both of us in our previous discussions. My imagination was immediately intrigued, concerned with imagined wild animalistic trains which crossed my mind, their tails twisting around and their maws wide open. Paradoxically, I came alive to this devastating image. Only after encountering the sense of terror coiled up in this fearful image of trains, I could recognize that both Danny and I were caught in an impasse for months. We liked each other but could not talk; emotional experiences were blocked. Sharing the dream was Danny's first time to connect to the fearful material and communicate it to me.

In response, I reminded Danny of the last time we were talking about trains. These were the trains which took his mother's family to the concentration camps. Danny's spontaneous and immediate response caught me by surprise. He said: "But my mother didn't catch the train. She told me that she missed it, that the train has left the station before her arrival."

Each psychodynamic endeavor has its own moments, and for us, this was the one. Indeed, it was preceded by a long period of not knowing where to go, but once the idiomatic expression "the train has left the station" was verbally pronounced, perpetual tardiness could be "touched." In Hebrew, Danny's language, the idiomatic expression is a more precise translation of his symptom, as by saying "to show up late to the train" we mean to miss opportunities. Danny's mother "missed" the train, she showed up late, and so she did not take the train to Auschwitz. Whereas usually people who "show up late to the train," whose train has already left the station, miss something, in Danny's family, this idiomatic expression carried the opposite meaning. By missing the train, his mother was saved from something so gruesome, so horrifying, that words cannot express it; Auschwitz is beyond words. For Danny's mother, therefore, being rescued was beyond imagination. What does it mean to miss the train to Auschwitz? How could a Jewish girl miss such a train? What exactly happened in these dark days in history, and how could a Jewish girl arrive too late to the train station, an act to which she owed her life? Danny did not have the answers to these questions. Actually, who does? Like many other Holocaust stories, they remained unexplainable. The idea of merging the experience of life with words such as "missing" and "showing up late" is undoubtedly a surprising combination, unique to Danny's relational world, a world in which arriving late may save a life. How exactly? Who knows? Such experiences are beyond logic.

Linking tardiness with saving a life was not accessible to us before Danny said that his mother was late for the train. Once it was overtly vocalized, using the well-known and deeply ingrained idiomatic expression so familiar in Hebrew, we could learn more about Danny's distinctive symptom. For Danny, being "good" meant remaining detached from his family's unspeakable past experiences. The same was true for our therapy; being "good" meant staying away from this kind of experience. The delay we experienced was the price we paid, but we needed this time to re-experience and reconstruct a relational matrix in which the only way to survive was by keeping a distance from life.

Living in the shadow of the Holocaust is not strange to me. As a Jew, born and residing in Israel, I used to imagine throughout my childhood how it might have felt "if I were there." I shared these attempts with my peers in a "collective experience" of children trying to comprehend the past of a previous generation. In this case, I am using the term "Social Unconscious" (Hooper and Weinberg, 2011).[1] There are several ways to understand this concept, but here I adopt the description which refers to the repressed parts of the psyche that people of the same society share without being aware of it.[2] I mention it since it took me a while to realize that at the same time Danny was manifesting an idiosyncratic, private pattern, he was also communicating something that we both shared as members of same society, and which cannot speak its mind. Moreover, it enabled me a closer contact with the untouchable. Paradoxically, being apparently "detached" was the most meaningful way by which to communicate the deepest meanings of being a second generation of Holocaust survivors. While neither Danny nor I could imagine this past, being detached together appeared to be an intimate communicative experience.

Staying long enough in such a relationship was my only way to learn how it feels to be so emotionally disconnected, and how dangerous it seems to take risks and create emotional contacts that might erode the sense of a safe place. It was also my way to learn about Danny's relational idiosyncratic meanings of tardiness. Being worried one session after another while waiting for his arrival, and then feeling relieved when reassured time and time again that nothing bad had happened to him, colored his tardiness with a unique meaning with which I became identified and took an active part in reconstructing the narrative of surviving an unknown and extreme threat. Paradoxically, Danny's tardiness was the only feature where he was not detached. Alongside the apparently distant mood, being late time after time functioned as an impactful way of communication, by which to unconsciously convey profound messages regarding Danny's relational world. The most communicative moments between us were those moments of Danny's absence. In so suggesting, I draw on the interest in the negative (Green, 1999) and the unrepresented (Levine, Reid and Scafone, 2013).

Many thinkers of the school of object relation, intersubjective and relational theories emphasized the idea that therapists have to wait long enough to allow an experience to emerge. Bollas used the phenomenon of mood to discuss it. He asserts that:

The psychoanalyst may allow for a substantial period of time to elapse before analyzing the patient's mood – and the Winnicottian and Kohutian sense of the need to allow for the patient's prolonged transference usage of the analyst as a self-object may be part of an implicit recognition that the analyst needs to establish a mood without premature challenge – it will become necessary at some time to reach the person while he is "inside" the mood . . . often this means contacting part of the individual's true self, but a true self that may be frozen in a developmental time when self-experience was traumatically arrested.
(Bollas, 1984, p. 210)

Bollas ascribes moods with a similar status to that of dreams in their ability to establish a mnemic environment in which the individual re-experiences and re-creates past infant-child experiences and states of being.

The dream was the venue by which to convey important messages regarding tardiness. Once it was possible to meet this material in the dream, it became available on the verbal level, and for the first time, we could discuss it between us. The new discourse allowed for new interpretations and meanings of trains in Danny's life.

Realizing an idiomatic expression

Danny's symptom was a precise translation of the idiomatic expression as appearing in Hebrew – his native tongue. In our new mode of discussion, it was possible to learn about his private language and its uniqueness within the general common slang. Whereas the idiomatic expression "the train has left the station" (in Hebrew: to be late for the train) usually carries negative meanings, in Danny's family, or at least the way Danny perceived it, it is a life-saving event. Showing up late for the train means avoiding something so gruesome, it is beyond words. Missing the train means avoiding devastation and annihilation. Indeed, session after session, Danny's tardiness revived something between us. What exactly? It seems as any hurried answer would miss the arc of narrative encapsulated in this enigmatically communicative symptom.

Though Danny's mother was rescued, the experience of mass eradication remained imprinted on the family's memory as an option that not only could happen in the past but could still occur any minute, threatening to destroy the family unless a miracle happens. And a miracle could happen if the train has left the station.

It is unclear how the idiomatic expression linking trains with tardiness became canonic in the Hebrew slang, as well as in other languages. It is unclear why it stands for the sense of missing. What is clear is that the fast moving train symbolizes, in this context, a place everyone travels collectively, to a defined destination and with a prescribed track, and whoever is late – loses. Both Freud and Jung assumed that the non-verbal levels of mental organization manifest themselves by symbols – visual representations including memories, experiences and emotions. However, whereas Freud's foregrounding of sexuality viewed trains moving in dreams as tantamount to sexual intercourse, Jung parts company with this emphasis on sexual drive and has placed the collective unconscious, with its archetypical symbols, in the heart of mental life.

In any case, the unique language of the human psyche manifests itself in many articulated forms. Danny is quite a communicative, verbal person. He could beautifully and clearly recount many of his life events, yet his behavioral symptom – his perpetual tardiness – was his unique way to communicate an idea which carries deep meanings, associated with primary experiences. In adult life, only vague repercussions of these far and removed experiences are echoed. Whereas his verbal language was fluent, ample, clear but not "touching," the non-verbal language operated in the opposite direction: it enigmatically preserved the experience in its idiosyncratic fashion, while the events and situations it represented remained veiled. The idiomatic expression "the train has left the station" (or when literally translated from Hebrew: to miss to train, to show up late for the train) was, in this case, a junction in whom the symbolic verbal mode of expression and the somatic-behavioral one consolidated. Danny's perpetual tardiness concretely illustrates the symbolic interpretation of this idiom. Developmental research (e.g., Bauer, 2004) describes the infant's pre-verbal capacity for representing patterns of interaction in the external world before explicit forms of memory begin to function, and before any symbolic description of such interaction is formulated. Although the ability and propensity to learn the language and use it in the service of imagination and communication are likely to be innate for the human species in general and as individuals, at some point of the development the meaning of specific words, expressions and idioms are often repressed and split off. Thus, such processes belong to the dynamic unconscious of individuals, intertwined with the dynamic Social Unconscious. In the case of our dyad relationship, Danny's symptom provided an opposite meaning to an idiom by which I was extremely impacted, as I usually fear to "miss trains." While Danny had his private connection to the trains, it was also a part of the social experience of the Holocaust. Understanding what the subject meant for Danny helped me find a unique interpretation of the social trauma for which I had no words at all.

Danny's immediate response after sharing the dream put into words the facts that his mother had formulated. In so doing, the two languages – the primary-somatic and the verbal-symbolic could be bridged, while the idiomatic expression could be deciphered in both languages, holding two poles – concrete and metaphoric. No wonder that the dream made this possible. In so asserting, I am using Freud's concepts not only regarding the unique status of dreams as a "royal road to the unconscious," but also the different types of thought processes that are blended in the dream "language." Furthering the understanding of therapists' witnessing patients' traumatic memories, Reis conceives witnessing as involving a phenomenon of memory, in what Loewald (1976) termed its *enactive representational form* (Reis, 2009, p. 1360). Reis focuses on the importance of allowing and witnessing memory in its varied forms,

> without attempting to symbolize or make personally understandable the experience – to accept the experience of trauma, without therapeutic ambition. The analyst occupying the position of the witness in a treatment understands that performative and enactive features of traumatic experience are not to be simply translated or transduced into symbolic form, and that a part of the integrity of the experience of trauma is itself its wordless registration.
>
> (p. 1360)

In the spirit of my book, I use Reis' quotation as an opportunity to clarify the way I combine Freud's early idea regarding the affinity between language and somatic symptoms, and the relational emphasis on the shared co-creation of experience between patient and therapist.

Reis concurs with Freud, who emphasized the non-conscious form of traumatic memory, and its quality as an action, suggesting that memory in hysterical neurosis was linked to motor reaction (Freud, 1895, p. 297), an approach that was later validated in contemporary cognitive science.[3] Freud (1914) also described the enactive qualities of the patient's traumatic reliving in the clinical setting: "He reproduces it not as a memory, but as an action; he repeats it, without, of course, knowing that he is repeating it" (p. 150). Freud demonstrated that the patient was not repeating a dissociated or repressed memory, but rather that the action of repetition itself was a mode of memory phenomena. "As long as the patient is in the treatment he cannot escape from this compulsion to repeat; and in the end we understand that this is his way of 'remembering'" (Freud, 1914, p. 150).

Following these ideas, Danny's symptom can be easily seen as a form of traumatic memory, linked to motor reaction, or, more precisely, behavioral pattern, in which additional remembering is seen as an act of repeating. This is linked to Freud's idea of the affinity between language and symptom, as Danny's behavior hides an idiomatic expression. However, for this to be deciphered and utilized, Danny needed an "Other" to witness it, to be there long enough so that his behavior would attain a relational meaning. To the early Freudian notion that views repetitive action as a form of memory, an additional aspect should be regarded – that of relational perspective. I had to let myself take an active part in the scene so that feelings of deep worry when he was late, and then the relieving feeling of "coming back to life" while he was showing up late to our sessions, would color Danny's tardiness in its unique quality, and load it with his idiosyncratic meanings. Whereas Freud described the enactive qualities of patient's traumatic reliving in the clinical setting, repeating it time and again, object-relation theory, as well as intersubjective and relational approaches, would emphasize the need for an active witness, i.e., the therapist, to allow a new experience to emerge. Both approaches emphasize the unconscious. However, adopting a relational view, my "idiosyncratic" response to Danny's tardiness was part of the enterprise of revealing its unique meaning. In addition, the way both of us feared close contact, was also part of our co-created experience. Danny's tardiness was not new; on the contrary, it was constant, repetitive, resistant and chronic. However, an active, present witness was needed to provide it with its relational meaning. First, without interpreting it, just letting it be. Later on, it became possible to harness my own subjective responses to the therapeutic process.

In Danny's relational world, this idiomatic expression has attained a surprising, opposite meaning from the one we generally expect. Not only that you do not miss anything if you miss the train, it is the only way to make life possible. This unique, private language, hidden even from Danny himself, was encrypted in his symptom. Using this language in its behavioral form was Danny's way to being saved over and over. It was his escape from an ongoing, predicted disaster. Every day in which he missed that train, he was repeatedly saved from sharing the fate of his mother's family and with millions of other Jews who, unfortunately, did catch the train. Day after day he rescued himself from an unknown, uncivilized, wild and ancient fate that cannot be expressed in words.

Reis suggests that:

> enactive memory phenomena in their bodily registration represent the essential force of traumatic occurrence, contained in a form of memory that may only be experienced as an event rather than narration. Thus, what are often regarded to be gaps or lacunae in the verbal, declarative memory of history [. . .] can be reconceptualized as experiences held in episodic memory systems that have no translation into language, but which convey the patients' modes of reaction as memory.
>
> (Reis, 2009, p. 1362)

In Danny's case, traumatic memories of the past generation are behaviorally registered by an individual who was not part of the scene, but "behaviorally remembers" an unspoken history of mass trauma. What makes Reis' idea so interesting in this specific case, is that this form of memory which "can only be experienced as event rather than narration" does have a symbolic linguistic pole, if we decipher the very familiar idiomatic expression hidden behind the patient's symptom and realized by his behavior. Its connection to the verbal realm is enigmatically encapsulated in the behavioral symptom. This way, a bridge is created, but to cross it, we first need to identify it. Carefully studying Danny's relational world, and then waiting for the moment to appear, could lead to the form of communication that would reach both modes of thoughts and being.

Coining the term "The Unthought Known," Christopher Bollas refers to experiences that are known to the individual, but about which he or she had not yet thought (Bollas, 1987). The Unthought Known may be viewed as expanding Winnicott's concept of true self. It refers to preverbal, unschematized early experiences that may determine one's behavior unconsciously, barred to conscious thought.

Bollas relates the human subjects' recording of his early experiences of the object. He takes from Freud while using the phrase "The Shadow of the Object" to discuss the process of internalization: "This is the shadow of the object as it falls on the ego, leaving some trace of its existence in the adult" (Freud, 1917, pp. 237–258, in Bollas, 1987, p. 3). The object can cast its shadow without a child being able to process this relation through mental representations or language. We should inquire what kind of environment Danny revived in his behavior. According to Bollas, some moods may represent a breakdown in the individual's self-development, in such a way that self-states released in a mood are acts of conservation and protest.

Moods are often the existential registers of the moment of a breakdown between a child and his parents, and partly notate the parent's own developmental arrest, in that the parent is unable to deal appropriately with the child's particular maturational needs. What was a self-experience in the child on that could have been integrated into the child's continuing self-development, was rejected by the parents, who failed to perform adequately as ordinary "transformational objects," thereby destining a self-state to be frozen by the child into a conservative object that fated such a state of being to be subsequently represented only through moods.

(Bollas, 1984, p. 211)

Danny's symptom enabled him to remain at home with his family, to recreate the family environment and conserve something that was, but no longer is. In Bollas's terminology, we may refer such symptom as "conservative object."

A conservative object is a being state preserved intact within a person's internal world: it is not intended to change and act as a mnemic container of a particular self-state conserved because it is linked to the child self's continuing negotiation with some aspect of the early parental environment. A child not only stores his experiences of an object, in that process we term internalization, but he also conserves self-states which may eventually become permanent features of his character. Further, the internal world is not simply composed of self and object representations; if it were, mental life would be restricted to that which can be symbolized through the creation of the object, a child may be enduring an experience which is registered not through object representation but through a kind of identity sense.

(Bollas, 1984, pp. 208–209)

Danny's repetitive compulsion yielded by this Unthought Known experiences governed his everyday life. Like other object relation thinkers, Bollas transformed the idea of the unconscious from an internal concept into an experience which is allowed to emerge by the Other. The Other is the transformative object, responsible for the emergence of experience, known as a mood, a dream or passion, but cannot be thought of.

Gradually, Danny and I could talk about his place and the way he was situated in his parents' life. For them, he represented a way to grasp life, to save them from mourning and loss. Unlike their many other relatives, who unfortunately did catch that train, he would never catch it; he would miss it day after day. In so doing, he has taken an active part in the mechanisms which could stop time. Unspoken past traumatic experiences were operating in the infrastructure of his experience, manifesting themselves behaviorally and concretely. That dark historical era needed to be left behind, and Danny was "assigned" the task of continuing life from the point in which other lives were cut off. Another "Other" had to be there to allow this experience to transform. I had to find my way of being with Danny, to carefully listen to his unique mode of communication. It seemed that until that turning point in therapy, in which the experience of the dream could be verbally rendered, Danny's repetition compulsion of the pattern of missing the train has not gone through symbolization.

Thinkers who followed the works of Klein and Bion have already related to the way in which symptoms may be viewed as metaphors to mental states. Some of them furthered more specifically the understanding of different levels of concretization and abstraction related to mental processes and symptoms. For example, McDougall describes the case of Tim, who as a young boy had one ideal: to be "heartless" (McDougall, 1989). This ideal found its expression in the actual inability to feel any emotion – pain, pleasure or any other feelings. Only after a prolonged period of therapy, and after Tim had suffered from myocardial infarction (a heart attack), did McDougall finally understand that for Tim, at least, the expression "heartless" was not only metaphoric but might also carry with it tragic implications. This led her to reconsider the entire therapeutic process. Tim's case is just one example wherein McDougall observed somatic illness as a metaphoric expression for mental disturbances, which appear when the individual's mental coping system collapses. This view, which deals with the affinity between the somatic, mental and verbal aspects of the human psyche, is part of the clinical practice. And yet, while McDougall describes a type of verbal expression that has a direct connection to a physiological phenomenon, her ideas are in line with many other analytical attempts to place the earliest impressions in life outside the symbolic/linguistic zone.

Even though many psychoanalysts have discussed the affinity between language and somatic sensations, it appears that since the age of Freud, the particular phenomenon of idiomatic expressions has yet to attain its deserved attention. In the project I shared with Yoav Yigael (Raufman and Yigael, 2010; 2011) we viewed idiomatic expressions as characterized by unique features that differentiate them from other metaphoric phenomena, especially in their ability to bridge the gap between somatic sensations and mental representations. McDougall, like other theoreticians, assumes that primary levels of mental organization have no representation in language. These conceptualizations show a distinct awareness of possible connections between somatic experiences and verbal expressions but still view the earliest somatic area as being pre-verbal.

During the pre-verbal stage of development, the baby experiences many diverse mental situations and acquires skills without using language. Many scholars, including Piaget, Bowlby and Stern, studied this stage of life. However, it seems that regarding the existence of primary levels of thought in an adult's mental life, many questions remain unanswered. To what extent can direct observations, made in early childhood, reach the integration and conceptualization of primary mental organization? What can we learn from the knowledge accumulated in early childhood about the existence of this level in adult life? How much can the therapist learn about these pre-verbal levels by reconstructing the origins of mental difficulties? Is the claim that these levels cannot be accessed through language after language has already been acquired, really true? Finding the answers to these questions is difficult. However, when an apparently bizarre and perplexing symptom attains meaning after deciphering a verbal realm operating underneath, a contact with more primary levels is allowed.

Gradually, Danny developed a growing interest in his family's history, during both therapy and life in general. He no longer approached the discussions as a bystander, passively absorbing the family history. Instead, he started to take an active part, to identify his feelings and his private emotional responses. This was part of a comprehensive development, in which he was more curious about his inner world and his relations with other people. Originally, his wife referred him to therapy, but progressively Danny could own this process, identify his needs and use it in his subjective way. To one of our sessions, he appeared almost on time, carrying a wrapped present, in which there was a nice big clock. "I'm aware that you already have two clocks in your clinic. However, mine is different. It is always five minutes late . . .".

Notes

1   Hopper and Weinberg (2011) also thoroughly discuss the difference between the group analytic concept of the Social Unconscious, relevant to a specific society, and the Jungian collective unconscious, universal and common to all human beings, although modern Jungians refer to cultural unconscious (Henderson, 1984) and cultural complex (Singer and Kimbles, 2004).
2   The idea implied in this concept is that the extents to which we are both restrained and constrained by the society in which we live is sometimes way

beyond what we imagine. It is possible to refer to this phenomenon as the "Social Unconsciousness," not because the material (facts/events) is necessarily unconscious, but rather because we are not necessarily aware of the ways and extent of its influence upon us.

3   Reis points out that when Freud and Breuer addressed the motor phenomena of hysterical attacks they wrote in the preliminary communication that these "can be interpreted partly as universal forms of reaction appropriate to the affect accompanying the memory . . . partly as a direct expression of these memories" (Breuer and Freud, 1893, p. 15, in Reis, 2009, p. 1360). Reis further asserts that the mnemic traces described by Freud as distributed physiological and non-conscious phenomena are more recently appearing as the enactive (Bruner, Oliver and Greenfield, 1966) subsymbolic (Bucci, 1997) procedural (Clyman, 1991) and implicit (Lyons-Ruth, 1998) encoding of information. Within contemporary psychoanalysis this pre-symbolic sensory-dominated mode of experiencing has led to basic conceptions of self-experiencing emphasizing rhythmicity and experiences of sensory contiguity organized at the level of sensory impression (Ogden, 1989). These experiences are memory without form, which, just as they inform, fall back into indeterminacy (Clough, 2007).

References

Balint, M. (1968). *The Basic Fault*. London: Tavistock.

Bauer, P. (2004). Getting Explicit Memory off the Ground: Steps toward Construction of a Neuro-Developmental Account of Changes in the First Two Years of Life, *Developmental Review*, 24: 347–373.

Bollas, C. (1984). Moods and the Conservative Process, *The International Journal of Psychoanalysis*, 65: 203–212.

Bollas, C. (1987). *The Shadow of the Object: Psychoanalysis of the Unthought Known*. New York: Columbia University Press.

Breuer, J. and Freud, S. (1893). On the Psychical Mechanism of Hysterical Phenomenon: A Preliminary Communication. In: J. Strachey (Ed. and Trans.) (1957), *The Standard Edition of the Complete Psychological Works of Sigmund Freud, Vol. 2*. London: Hogarth Press.

Bruner, J.S., Oliver, R.R. and Greenfield P.M. (1966). *Studies in Cognitive Growth*. New York: Wiley.

Bucci, W. (1997). *Psychoanalysis and Cognitive Science: A Multiple Code Theory*. New York: Guilford.

Clough, P.T. (2007). Introduction. In: P.T. Clough and J. Halley (Eds.), *The Affective Turn*. Durham, NC: Duke University Press, pp. 1–33.

Clyman, R.B. (1991). The Procedural Organization of Emotions: A Contribution from Cognitive Science to the Psychoanalytic Theory of Therapeutic Action, *Journal of American Psychoanalytic Association*, 39: 349–381.

Freud, S. (1895). The Psychotherapy of Hysteria. In: J. Strachey (Ed. and Trans.) (1957), *The Standard Edition of the Complete Psychological Works of Sigmund Freud, Vol. 2*. London: Hogarth Press.

Freud, S. (1914). Remembering, Repeating, and Working Through. In: J. Strachey (Ed. and Trans.) (1958), *The Standard Edition of the Complete Psychological Works of Sigmund Freud, Vol. 12*. London: Hogarth Press.

Frued, S. (1917). Mourning and Melancholia. In: J. Strachey (Ed. and Trans.) (1957), *The Standard Edition of the Complete Psychological Works of Sigmund Freud, Vol. 14*. London: Hogarth Press.

Green, A. (1999). *The Work of the Negative*. A. Weller (Trans.). London: Free Association Books.

Grossmark, R. (2012). The Unobtrusive Relational Analyst, *Psychoanalytic Dialogues*, 22: 629–646.

Henderson, J.L. (1984). *Cultural Attitudes in Psychological Perspective*. Toronto: Inner City Books.

Loewald, H.W. (1976). Perspectives on Memory. In: *The Essential Loewald: Collected Papers and Monographs*. Hagerstown, MD: University Publishing Group, pp. 148–173.

Levine, H., Reed, G.S and Scarfone, D. (2013). *Unrepresented States and the Construction of Meaning. Clinical and Theoretical Contributions*. London: Karnac.

Lyons-Ruth, K. (1998). Implicit Relational Knowing: Its Role in Development and Psychoanalytic Treatment. *Infant Mental Health Journal*, 19: 282–289.

Hopper, E. and Weinberg, H. (Eds.) (2011). *The Social Unconscious in Persons, Groups, and Societies, Vol I*. London: Karnac.

McDougall, J. (1989). *Theatres of the Body: A Psychoanalytic Approach to Psychosomatic Illness*. New York: Norton.

Ogden, T.H. (1989). *The Primitive Edge of Experience*. Northvale, NJ: Aronson.

Raufman, R. and Yigael, Y. (2010). "Feeling Good in Your Own Skin," Part I: Primary Levels of Mental Organization, *American Journal of Psychoanalysis*, 70: 361–385.

Raufman, R. and Yigael, Y. (2011). "Feeling Good in Your Own Skin," Part II: Idiomatic Expressions: The Language's Way to Connect with the Primary Levels of Mental Organization, *American Journal of Psychoanalysis*, 71: 16–36.

Reis, B. (2009). Performative and Enactive Features of Psychoanalytic Witnessing: The Transference as the Scene of Address, *International Journal of Psychoanalysis*, 90: 1359–1372.

Singer, T. and Kimbles, S. (Eds.) (2004). *The Cultural Complex: Contemporary Jungian Perspectives on Psyche and Society*. London: Brunner-Routledge.

Slochower, D. (1996). Holding: Something Old and Something New. In: L. Aron and A. Harris (Eds.), *Relational Psychoanalysis, Vol II: Innovation and Expansion*. Hillsdale, NJ: The Analytic Press.

Slochower, D. (2004). *Holding and Psychoanalysis: A Relational Approach*. Hillsdale, NJ: The Analytic Press.

Chapter 3

What's the matter?

One major challenge of the clinical enterprise is how to use words in a way that touches primary, sensorial, non-verbal experiences. How could the symbolic language reach those ancient layers of the human psyche, which had not yet gone through symbolization and were not verbally encoded? And how could the "primary psyche" put itself into words, by which to tell about its condition?

A few years ago, a young adolescent was referred to my clinic. Shirley and her family were recent immigrants from the United States, and the girl was struggling with extreme emotional and social issues, probably intensified by the vulnerability usually characterizing her age group. Shirley's parents felt that she needed reassurance and support, especially because of their immigration and adjustment difficulties. Pretty soon, however, it became apparent that Shirley's problems could not be attributed to these circumstances, but were much deeper.

Whenever she entered my consulting room, she would gaze into space. She partly saw me, partly ignored me, as if I were a foreign body in her field of vision which she needed to adjust to, or possibly get rid of. Later on, I learned how complex my presence was for her, but for several sessions, I found it extremely difficult to understand her world. Shirley reminded me of the Little Prince, a native of another planet. It was more than the fact that we were not well acquainted yet; her arrival from abroad and her immigrant status were not a mere geographic fact. Rather, it felt as if she indeed arrived "from another planet," and we had to start learning each other's languages. Privately, I wondered about her early experiences. Did anyone else find it difficult to understand Shirley? How did she feel amidst such lack of comprehension?

When Shirley mentioned she found it difficult to express herself in Hebrew, I suggested she could speak English whenever she pleased, and alternate between the languages as needed. But her difficulties were not merely a matter of verbal language; they had a deeper origin of finding an emotional way of expression. This presented a conundrum: when she said that expressing herself in Hebrew was hard, did she mean that the common language spoken *here*, in my country, was hard because Shirley belonged *there*, in the country she left behind? Or perhaps she was telling me that the language I was using as a psychologist, the language of the psyche, was not familiar to her? Did speaking the psychic language feel like something from an alien planet?

At this point, I want to mention the need to acknowledge how speech creates performative action between therapist and patient. Reis draws on this topic as part of his attempts to expand the notion of witnessing in therapy and allow the idea of witnessing to encompass the relational event which occurs in the transference–countertransference matrix (Reis, 2009). Reis takes the concept from the philosopher J.L. Austin (1962), who

> conceived of the uses of speech beyond its declarative function in the development of speech act theory. Austin drew attention to the usages of language that went beyond the making of factual assertions, to perform actions. In these instances, speech is itself considered a form of action, or, as Austin quipped: "by saying something we do something."
>
> (Reis, 2009, p. 1363)

One recurring theme during my work with Shirley was her response to my physical presence. At a certain point, she stopped gazing into space. She seemed unable to take her eyes off me and actually started staring at me. She often commented on my looks, paying attention to every detail – what I wore, my bag, my shoes – and asking many questions, such as: Do you like wearing dresses? Are these shoes new?

Apparently, Shirley did not associate these questions with our therapeutic sessions. Like her, these questions "did not belong" to our shared realm, to the here-and-now of our relations. They seemed to "replace" the topic we were supposed to discuss. What sort of therapist discusses her dresses and shoes with her patients?

However, these questions became, unerringly, the channels connecting us. Pronounced in a foreign accent, and seemingly coming from "another planet," Shirley's inquiries brought her to life in my room. She became vivacious and inquisitive and caught as I was in her gaze, I also came alive and present. The shared realm of our meetings had started to unfold, alternating between estrangement and alliance. At that point, I was satisfied by her attention to the details of my appearance and started noticing the way she dressed, did her hair, and other details of her appearance. For example, I was intrigued by the fact that although she declared she did not like pink, she usually wore this color to our meetings. It was as if her clothes were not necessarily a part of her, but a foreign object she brought to our sessions. I commented that sometimes we say things that do not necessarily harmonize with what we do.

At the end of one session, Shirley was standing by the door, finding it difficult to say goodbye. Suddenly she started talking to me in a tone I did not hear before; something that I felt is special for her, revealing a new, probably surprising emotion. She asked me: "Ravit, what is your meter?"

Approaching me directly by mentioning my name was a new mode of expression in our discourse. It turned out that, curious about my height, she wanted to ask how tall I was. Was I one meter and sixty centimeters tall? Or one meter and seventy centimeters tall? What exactly was "my meter?"

I was accustomed to Shirley's use of my physical parameters to organize my image, to enable me a place in her world, to internalize something of me. While endeavoring to understand what she was trying to ask, I just answered her question, as if willing to join the game.

Nevertheless, it was clear that her question touched a very deep internal layer of her experience. The incorrect syntax of the phraseology – "What is your meter?" – instead of asking how tall I was, aroused an intensely personal response in me. Shirley was deviating from formal language, and creating something different; it is possible to suggest that this is how a new immigrant talks. However, it is the "incorrect" language, the creation of a personal language of her own that relates to my appearance in the room, evoking such a strong feeling. It was a feeling that was not trapped or fixated by words and was not forced to fit into the demanding social linguistic system. The motion and shifts between different kinds of languages created by Shirley were not experienced at that moment as a limitation or a barrier. Instead, it seemed to enable something new to emerge. It opened a space where we could reach new and hidden psychic areas. In her book *Cleft Tongue* (2014) Dana Amir touches upon the psychic language and its diverse forms and modes of expression, "both within psychic structures as well as the inter-personal realm" (p. xi). She addresses patients who are incapable of establishing a psychic language which includes abstracted images and symbols. The only language available for them is a concrete one. Amir further stresses that "the establishment of a pseudo-language is not just the only way of preventing contact – but also the only way to preserve it" (p. 25). She explains how the non-existence of things within language "not only bars us from contact with them but is paradoxically also the only way of keeping them hidden" (pp. 25–26). In one of her clinical illustrations she shows how "Psychotic thinking or psychotic syntax is actually a way to preserve thinking through non-thinking" (p. 109). The interplay between Hebrew and English opened up a playful way for in-between experiences. I inferred that maybe by asking me "what is my meter" Shirley actually asking me: "What's the matter?" Or: "What's the matter with you?"

While describing his encounter with the Little Prince, Antoine De Saint-Exupery beautifully illustrates how meaningful encounters with individuals he deems he can really talk to do not occur in a planned manner and are not formally constructed. Instead, the pilot's truthful connection with the Little Prince and his rescue from loneliness transpire by accident. In the novel, the pilot states that he had lived his life alone, lacking someone that he could *really* talk to, until he had an accident with his plane in the Sahara Desert, when his engine developed trouble and he was forced to make difficult repairs all on his own, lacking a mechanic or passengers (1977, p. 7).

Shirley and I were standing by the door, visually estimating each other's height. I told her that last time I measured myself I was one meter seventy tall. And then, after a pause, words came unbidden to my lips and I heard myself asking: "And what's the matter with you?"

She thought for a minute and replied: "I am not sure. Something is bothering me." And after a pause, she added: "and I am one-meter fifty-three."

Her natural, spontaneous reply to my question testified to the body's involvement in the establishment of language. Shirley and I could speak about height and mood by using the same word, which was emptied of its original linguistic meaning and given a new one, loaded with physical sensation. It was as if each centimeter in our bodies revealed something about our "meters" and "matters" in both linguistic and non-linguistic mode. Also, my "meter," while it may be regarded as an objective fact since I am indeed one meter and seventy tall, had attained a new meaning when reflected in Shirley's gaze. The same was probably true for my "matter" – my willingness to be affected by Shirley's subjectivity. While writing these lines, it occurred to me that the words "meter" and "matter" are phonetically associated with the word "mother" as it sounds in Shirley's "mother's" tongue (English), as well as Mütter (German), mère (French), Mater (Latin), Moeder (African), Mèder (Bolognese and Irish), Madre (Italian), and Muter (Yiddish), among many other languages. Amir writes about the affinity between establishing language and the process of separation-individuation from the mother. She calls this process "from mother-tongue to language," asserting that

> language is first and foremost a depressive achievement of involving both the concession of what cannot be articulated – and the giving up of the symbiosis with the other by acknowledging him or her as a distinct subject. Indeed, acknowledging separation is simultaneously the driving motivation to speak as well as an essential condition for establishing language.
>
> (2014, p. 1)

Following this, and as illustrated in other chapters of this book, rebelling against structural linguistic rules by creating an idiosyncratic language is often associated with a search for new ways of being and new experiences to emerge. Amir quotes Kristeva, who describes a patient who uses language as armor to protect himself from her presence and interventions. As a child who went unseen by his mother – he now goes on not seeing her. He calls his mother "the mother" rather than "my mother," to avoid contact with his suppreessed intimacy with her (Kristeva, 1995, p. 11, in Amir, 2014, p. 3).

As opposed to using language to avoid contact, Shirley's mode of communication, especially the way she apparently "distorted" language by mixing the somatic (meter) with the symbolic (matter) – both resonating the word "mother" – felt as an impactful communicative gesture. She had to create contact with my physical body, similar to how babies, during early infancy, are first and foremost physically attached to their mothers. A close association with my physical existential parameters was needed for the establishment of the emotional connection, by which it was possible to say that "something was bothering her." This situation is opposite from the one described by Kristeva, in which the patient creates an "artificial discourse" based on logical and syntactical rules rather than on his own feelings and urges

> bringing about a fissure between the discourse's symbolic function and the concealed regions of his non-spoken drives, a fissure that manifests

itself through somatic symptoms. Instead of constituting an identity, his alienation from his body creates a self-sufficient totality that misses nothing, and therefore needs no one.
(Kristeva, 1995, p. 14, in Amir, 2014, p. 3)

According to Petrey (1990), speech acts perform a collectivity that can be as small as two people (e.g., analysand and analyst), but performative speech can never be the unilateral act of a single individual. Thus, for instance, the analyst's uttering the words "Our time is up for today" to the analysand is not merely a factual assertion, but performs an action within the community of the therapeutic dyad. Speech act theory may be seen to underlie Schafer's (1976) conception of an action language, as well as Ogden's (1994) concept of interpretive action. Both Loewald (1978) and Greenberg (1996) have also observed that words do not substitute or hold back action, but are actions in themselves.

Amir presents the conditions necessary for the creation of a living language, which "gives the interior a sense of measure but also maintains its quest after immortality . . . a language that is capable of transcending itself as well as of observing itself, one that enacts truth rather than just describing it" (2014, p. 3). Regarding the affinity between the capacity of creating a living language and the quality of maternal care, Amir further stresses that

> A discussion of the attacks on the creation of psychic language cannot bypass the question of the "mother-tongue" and its significance and influence on the child's ability to his or her own language. Does the mother-tongue constitute an emotional language that enables us to know and bear the insufferable, or does it haunt it, alienating itself from it? Does the mother welcome her infant's investigating gaze, or rather attack it and move it away?
>
> (p. 3)

In Shirley's case, it seems that the difficulty presented by her parents as "linguistic," triggered by the challenges of adjusting to her move to Israel, represented a much deeper issue in her capacity to communicate emotionally and to feel understood and seen. I am not hypothesizing here on her early relations with her mother. Rather, I strive to illustrate how co-creating our own shared language in the therapeutic enterprise was involved with profound aspects of our communication. Such a language resides on the border between the symbolic and the somatic, or the "semiotic" in Kristeva's terminology. While using fragments of symbolic language, it provided words with new meanings that could only be understood in the context of our relationship. A stranger would not have recognized that in our discourse, "meter" is associated with "matter" and both are connected with "mother." Object relation theories tend to compare therapist–patient relationships to that of parent–child. Following this reasoning, establishing emotional language was involved with the need for a deeper familiarity with my body for Shirley not only to internalize me, but also to set on a co-created experience in which both are part of a shared creation. For this to emerge, I also had to allow myself to "play" with Shirley, to free my own creativity and imagination in my response to her. Bromberg states that

> The relative presence of "imagination" in human discourse overlaps to no small degree with the relative capacity for intersubjectivity that exists in any relationship. The nature of the patient/therapist relationship in analytic treatment could thus be described as a journey in which two people must each loosen the rigidity of their dissociative "truths" about self and other in order to allow "imagination" to find its shared place.
>
> (2013, p. 1)

I suggest that by "dissociative truths" we may refer to the way we relate language and linguistic "truth" as well as our capacity to play with language. Creating a new language is associated with new self-states; co-creating it is thus associated with a newly shared self-states. As Bromberg puts it,

> As self-state permeability increases, so does openness to "state-sharing." The cocreation of a lived, relational unconscious more and more nourishes the willingness of each person to participate in a growing sense of "We" that includes "Me" and "You" as part of their individually expanded self-experiences. By living together in the enacted shadow of what is visible but not perceived, an opportunity is afforded to encounter what has been hidden in plain sight. If an analyst is emotionally and interpersonally alive as a partner while the different areas of a patient's developmental trauma are being relived safely but not too safely, the patient's threshold for the potential triggering of affect-dysregulation is raised at the brain level. This allows their relationship greater interpersonal spontaneity and creative self-expression that is carried by an expanded sense of selfhood into the world "out there."
>
> (p. 1)

The moment in which we stood looking at each other at the threshold of my consulting room, was a time of meeting. The reciprocal gaze enabled the creation of a language capable of describing in the same word an emotional experience ("What's the matter?") and a physical existence that could be measured by a look ("How meter tall are you?"). That look neither intruded nor ignored. Rather, it enabled the stitching together of experiences which are often riddled with holes, and weave, by the use of a single word, the body's contour with the internal psyche. When we say in English (as well as in other languages) "I see what you mean," we mean "I understand you." It denotes that seeing is tantamount to understanding. Following that session, in which Shirley and I developed our own unit of measurement that can size up both the body's contour and the psyche's depth, we went on a quest of developing our own language. For example, she told me that it took her a while to realize what it meant that when her peers in school use a word that sounded like "shoe" when addressing her. Eventually, she understood that they actually used an Arabic slang word, "shoo," which meant "How are you doing?" She commented: "It is strange. 'Shoe' is something you put on your foot." However, very soon she translated this new information into our new language, pointed at my shoes and asked in Arabic: "Shoo?" I replied that I am fine, and no, my shoes are not new, but I like them. We laughed.

A large body of material has already been dedicated to the role of metaphors in emotional experiences and the relations between body and language. A significant contribution to this emerges not only from psychoanalytic literature but also from philosophy and anthropology. George Lakoff and Mark Johnson suggested that our conscious world is ingrained in our physical entity and that the cognitive structure originates from the physical infrastructure of the nervous system. These scholars suggest that metaphor is not merely "a way of talking" in the conventional sense but rather a fundamental structure, which cannot be ignored and which penetrates into all our cognitive infrastructures on a symbolic level. Metaphor emphasizes the affinity between the imagination and the physical experience, where all the rules and structures start. The physical experience finds its way to the brain; thus the imagination is not merely perceived as a wild quality of fantasy and creativity, lacking all rules, but as having a physical basis (Johnson, 1987; Lakoff, 1987; Lakoff and Johnson, 1980).

Lakoff and Johnson deal with the affinity existing between our subjective world, as expressed by language, and our biological-human infrastructure, which is evolutional. Their argument states that most human language is metaphorical, based on images emerging from sensual-emotional contact with the human-material environment. At different levels of contact, categorization processes take place; they include conception, perception, processing and arrangement, most of which are sub-conscious and inconceivable on a conscious level. The scholars named these processes "the cognitive unconscious." Metaphors connect the concrete with the abstract, the sensual, the imaginative, the aesthetic and the emotional. The experience of the body within the world is central to the creation of metaphor.

A memory shared by one of my patients may well illustrate this idea. When her son was three years old, she took him to the graduation ceremony of a relative who had completed a training program in one of the military divisions. As part of the ceremony, the commanding officer of the military base and the commanding officer of the corps were invited to give their speech. Complete silence prevailed; everyone in the audience was waiting to hear the officers' speeches, when her son's voice was heard, loud and clear, "Look!" he shouted with astonishment, "the Base Commander is 'higher' than the Corps Commander!" The incident caused both embarrassment and amusement but not surprise, since in Hebrew, the word used by the boy, "gavoha," represents both "tall" and "high." In this particular case, the Corps Commander was, of course, higher in rank, but physically shorter than the Base Commander. According to the logic of a three-year-old child, the physical experience did not fit the social situation, and the infantile psyche immediately recognizes the paradox. It is not happenstance that children compare heights, competing who is "higher." The infantile psyche interprets the taller person as located higher in the social hierarchy. In very early stages of life, individuals are exposed to sensations and experiences related to their location in space. The experience of objects and figures around us which are higher or lower than us, at hand or not at hand, penetrable or impenetrable, and especially subjected or not subjected to our influence, is central in the establishment of selfhood.

Returning to Shirley, it seems that prior to being able to connect to her feelings and express them, she had to create contact with more primary, somatic aspects of experience. This idea was evident in her many questions regarding my body, my clothes and my general physical appearance. In a playful situation, such transitions from the concrete to the abstract, and the other way around, are possible.

In Lewis Carroll's literary masterpiece *Through the Looking Glass*, Alice tells the Red Queen that she can't find her way. The Red Queen furiously replies that she doesn't understand what Alice means by "her way," as all the "ways" belong to the Red Queen. Alice's lost way in the forest is concretely interpreted by the Queen, who is not capable of metaphoric thinking and metaphoric expressions such as "way of life." For the Queen, every way is within a physical or geographical territory which can be owned only by one single proprietor. For a co-created shared experience, an additional quality is required. The relations between Alice and the Queen exemplify what this lost way in the forest is missing in order to become a "way of life," or a way through the psychic metaphoric realm, in which it is possible to "progress," to "move" and to find a direction. The Queen's inability to emotionally communicate with Alice in a way that includes abstract layers of discourse deprives Alice of a potential partner needed for the establishment of psychic language and for the capacity to move between concrete and symbolic realms. She remains lost in the forest, where all ways belong to "Her Majesty."

Further illustrations of the ideas presented here are drawn from another vignette, taken from a therapy of another teenage patient named Gabi. Gabi could openly report her problematic interactions with her mother, characterized by violent confrontations and the underlying relentless feeling that her mother could not understand her. Under such constraints, Gabi felt she had to hide many things from her mother. She lived under the constant threat of imminent danger since she had no one to help her and protect her from the hazardous situations she had often brought upon herself, including unsafe relationships with men and hitch-hiking in the small hours of the night. She could not share these experiences with her mother, as she feared her mother would make her life even more miserable and imprison her at home. Within this hectic matrix, I found the situation extremely hard to handle. Not only was I bothered by the perilous experiences Gabi went through, but I knew that I had a professional obligation to report some of them. How was I to protect her at the same time I helped her find her own way?

One interesting part of our therapeutic relationship was a small recurring ritual, in which I went to make myself a cup of coffee and ask Gabi if she would like one too. After she replied positively, I used to ask her how she sweetened her coffee. In response, she always smiled, and I did not know why. It was only after several times of seeing her smile that I asked her for the meaning of it. She said that she enjoyed hearing me say the word "sweeten." Later she confessed that wanting me to ask her how to sweeten her drink was the only reason she accepted the offer of a cup of coffee. Hearing me pronounce the word "sweeten" sounded sweet to her, and I felt that when she told me about the facts she hid from her mother, she was "whispering sweet secrets" to me.

This was how I realized that her secrets sweetened her bitter reality. They created a sense of self that was not trampled upon by her mother in the judgmental world they inhabited, a world that did not allow Gabi enough space to grow. It is important to note, however, that the above description does not necessarily mean that she was a "bad mother" in any way. Rather, due to several problems, she was unable to comprehend her daughter's world.

The opportunity of alleviating Shirley's and Gabi's loneliness was associated with the option of creating a shared language; one that was not only informatively correct, but a living language, permitting us to speak our minds, communicate with each other and touch upon deep emotions. Learning their private language and exposing them to mine, so that together we created something new, was a process of establishing a living connection by which an experience of vitality could emerge both inside and outside the therapeutic sessions.

References

Amir, D. (2014). *Cleft Tongue: The Language of Psychic Structure*. London: Karnac.
Austin J.L. (1962). *How To Do Things with Words*. Cambridge, MA: Harvard University Press.
Bromberg, P.M. (2013). Hidden in Plain Sight: Thoughts on Imagination and the Lived Unconscious, *Psychoanalytic Dialogues*, 23: 1–14.
Carroll, L. (1872). *Through the Looking Glass*. London: Penguin.
de Saint-Exupery, A. (1977). *The Little Prince*. London: William Heinemann.
Schafer, R. (1976). *A New Language for Psychoanalysis*. New Haven, CT: Yale University Press.
Greenberg, J. (1996). Psychoanalytic Words and Psychoanalytic Acts: A Brief History, *Contemporary Psychoanalysis*, 32: 195–213.
Johnson, M. (1987). *The Body in the Mind: The Bodily Basis of Meaning, Imagination and Reason*. Chicago, IL and London: The University of Chicago Press.
Kristeva, J. (1995). *New Maladies of the Soul*. New York: Columbia University Press.
Lakoff, G. (1987). *Women, Fire and Dangerous Things. What Categories Reveal About the Mind*. Chicago, IL and London: The University of Chicago Press.
Lakoff, G. and Johnson, M. (1980). *Metaphors We Live By*. Chicago, IL and London: The University of Chicago Press.
Loewald, H.W. (1978). Primary Process, Secondary Process and Language. In: *The Essential Loewald: Collected Papers and Monographs*. Haggerstown, MD: University, pp. 87–101.
Ogden, T. (1994). The Concept of Interpretive Action, *Psychoanalytic Quarterly*, 63: 219–245.

Pine, F. (1981). In the Beginning: Contributions to a Psychoanalytic Developmental Psychology, *International Review of psychoanalysis*, 8: 15–33.

Petrey, S. (1990). *Speech Acts and Literary Theory*. New York: Routledge.

Reis, B. (2009). Performative and Enactive Features of Psychoanalytic Witnessing: The Transference as the Scene of Address, *The International Journal of Psychoanalysis*, 90: 1359–1372.

Chapter 4

Digging into the past

One of the most fascinating occurrences in the therapeutic enterprise is our ability to be impressed by the pictorial way by which human psyche manifests itself. When we weave the connecting thread between an image and the words it conceals, a powerful, influential intervention method emerges. We often use the word "impression" when relating to the ways events and experiences are *imprinted* on the psyche. The use of this word is neither a happenstance nor a coincidence.

Events experienced in early infancy, prior to the use of words, are deeply imprinted upon our heart as raw, crude feelings characterized by images, or by qualities associated with the senses such as smell or sound. This is why psychoanalysis emphasizes finding ways of using words that can echo the language of early impressions – that of images and senses. The case presented in this chapter serves to illustrate how the human psyche uses the language of images and senses to express itself. It also demonstrates the interplay between the two forms of language – the verbal/symbolic and the pictorial/concrete as it is often conducted in the therapeutic endeavor. This interaction is necessary for reaching the deep layers of the human psyche and bridging both languages to achieve a mental change.

A while ago, Michael was referred to my clinic due to a problem with which he had been struggling for years. He explained that he had better and worse times, but generally he had to deal with this issue daily and had suffered deeply. I do not intend to focus on the problem itself, but rather the healing methodology. The idea sounds absurd – how could we explain the healing without providing details regarding the problem? Nevertheless, my aim here is to illustrate a method which strives to reach the non-verbal levels of experience by the use of words. In so doing, we create interventions capable of echoing early states associated with primary life stages.

Michael linked the problems with the relations with his father very early in life. He described his father as a judgmental, detached man, who was never satisfied with Michael. "However, what's the point in recounting this fact over and over again?" Michael used to ask during our sessions; "I'm not going to sit on this couch for the rest of my life, complaining about my father. At a certain age, you must move on." This is a common statement, frequently raised in my clinic. I hear it from many patients who argue: "How much digging into the past is necessary?" Perhaps they are right. It is not enough to just talk about certain things. Something more is needed to achieve change. Speech should touch a deeper layer, not merely the verbal zone.

Michael grew up in a small settlement located in the south of the country. His mother was a homemaker, and his father was involved in the archaeological dig at a nearby excavation site. Pleasant memories regarding his father were always tied in with visits to the dig. He reminisced about the thrilling experience of exposing layers of Roman ruins, the joy of unearthing shards, spearheads, fossils and other historic and prehistoric treasures. These were happy days, redolent with the feeling of being a part of something bigger than himself. Even his father, who would walk around the dig wearing work clothes and ankle boots, transcended his individual existence and seemed to belong to something vast and primal. Michael was elated by these inspiring, uplifting thoughts.

All other memories of his father were a heavy burden, and he despaired not only of them but of his life in general. In particular, he was frustrated because at his mature age, and after so many years, these impressions still cast a dark shadow.

During our sessions, Michael shared diverse experiences that took place at different times of his life. It was fascinating to note that during his easier days, the days in which he felt relief, he invariably shared memories from the excavation site. A parallel was, therefore, created between the exposure of the layers of the Roman ruins at the excavation site his father worked on, and the uncovering of a layer within Michael's soul. The metaphoric meaning of the words "digging into the past," so often used in our daily vernacular, became connected to its most concrete sense in a way so impactful as to eventually assist in undoing one of the most permanent and resistant symptoms with which Michael was struggling. It was like turning ghosts into ancestors.

Connecting archaeology with deep emotions was not unique to Michael. Freud himself related to archaeology, and more specifically to Rome, stating that "our present ego-feeling is thus only a shrunken residue of a much more comprehensive – indeed, all-encompassing-feeling, which corresponded to a more intimate connection of the ego with the surrounding world" (Freud, 1930, p. 48). In his essay *Civilization and its Discontents* (1930) Freud addresses the question: May we assume that this primary ego-feeling has been preserved in the mental life of many people, and stands beside the more narrowly and sharply demarcated ego-feeling of maturity as a sort of counterpart? He presents an example taken from zoology:

> with animals we assume that the most developed species have proceeded from the lowest. But among living life forms, we still find all the simple ones today. The race of the great dinosaurs has died out and has made way for the mammals, but an actual representative of that race, the crocodile, is still living with us . . . in the realm of the mind, though, the preservation of the primitive beside what has developed from it through transformation is so frequent that there is no need to demonstrate this through examples.
>
> (p. 49)

This idea has attained various conceptualizations in throughout the years. However, its relevance to the mental realm and to the fact that the human's psyche consists of at least two different modes and layers, the primitive and the more developed, is irrefutable.

Michael was highly perturbed by a strange dilemma. How could a mature, highly self-aware individual with strong mental capacity such as himself, become trapped by a seemingly primordial entanglement with no means of escape? As for the preservation of the mind, Freud has argued that "in mental life nothing once formed can perish – that somehow everything is preserved and can, under suitable circumstances (e.g., through a sufficiently far-reaching regression), be brought to light again" (p. 49). Freud relates the concept of the preservation of the past to Rome, where various ancient portions still lie buried in the soil of the city, beneath its modern buildings (p. 50). He suggests that

> Rome is not a place of human habitation but a mental entity with a similarly long and rich past- an entity then, in which nothing that has once occurred has disappeared, and in which all earlier developmental phases, continue to exist.

Freud's choice of Rome as the representation of the realm of the mind is especially interesting in light of the connection created by Michael, more than a hundred years later, between the digging of Roman ruins and his psychic experiences in "digging into his past." While Michael resisted the need to "dig into his past," the most concrete meaning of the experience of digging had often been raised in our therapeutic enterprise, emotionally loaded, and charged with mostly positive associations related to his early childhood. Michael's revelations of his childhood feeling, as they coincided with the exposure of the Roman ruins, and then combining them with Freud's descriptions, helped me clarify what was needed in Michael's healing process. In our daily slang, we use the idiom "to dig into the past" to describe an exaggerated preoccupation with past experiences, or with experience in general. Equally, we may say that an incorrect style of digging at an excavation site might damage, sabotage or wreck the process of exposing the historical findings. Failing to choose the exact location, missing the right angle of digging or miscalculating the intensity of the encounter of the spade with the ground might destroy the fragile shards. In the therapeutic enterprise, misinterpreting, inaccurate observations and lack of courageous interventions might miss important evidence and leave essential parts of the "ruins" obscured by dust. Like archaeological digs at the excavation site, digging into the past in therapy must be done carefully, gently and handled with courage. What is even more interesting, is that similar to Michael's relations with his father, Freud described his attitude toward Rome in terms of approach–avoidance conflict, calling it a "neurotic desire." In his book *Freud: A Life for Our Time*, Peter Gay writes about Freud's intense relationship with Rome:

> Perhaps the most intriguing, certainly among the most poignant of the clues to his mind that Freud scattered through *The Interpretation of Dreams* is the theme of Rome, glittering in the distance as supreme prize and incomprehensible menace. It was a city that he had been avid to visit, but he found his desire strangely subverted by a kind of phobic prohibition. He took vacations in Italy more than once but got no nearer to Rome than Lake Trasimeno, about fifty miles away. This was the place where Hannibal, too, had stopped short.
>
> (1998, p. 132)

Similar to the qualities of Michael's relations with his father, Freud also conceptualized his relations to Rome in terms of Oedipal qualities. Gay writes:

> In late 1897, he dreamt that he and Fliess might hold one of their "congresses" in Rome, and in early 1899, he played with the idea of

meeting there at Easter, it struck him as a splendid idea, he wrote later that year, "to hear of the eternal laws of life first in the Eternal City." He studied the topography of Rome in what he called a torment of yearning, aware that there was something distinctly odd about his obsession. "By the way," he told Fliess, "my longing for Rome is deeply neurotic. It is connected with my schoolboy enthusiasm for the Semitic hero Hannibal."

(p. 132)

Gay reminds us that Freud interpreted this attitude as an expression of his passionate wish to defy and defeat anti-Semites:

To conquer Rome was to triumph in the seat – the very headquarters – of the Jews' most implacable enemies: Hannibal and Rome symbolized for the youth the contrast between the tenacity of Jewry and the organization of the Catholic church. There was more to it even than that; his desire for Rome, he noted, stood as 'cloak and symbol for several other hotly longed-for wishes.' They were, he hinted, Oedipal in nature; he recalled the ancient oracle given to the Tarquins that he who first kissed the mother would become the ruler of Rome.

(p. 132)

Gay further asserts that "A charged and ambivalent symbol, Rome stood for Freud's most potent concealed erotic, and only slightly less concealed aggressive wishes, and lanced at their secret history" (p. 132). By September 1901, Freud, at last, overcame his long-standing inhibition and was visiting Rome. Gay writes that "Like many northerners first entering Rome . . . he walked about wrapped in a daze of delight. Christian Rome disturbed him, modern Rome seemed promising and congenial, but it was ancient and Renaissance Rome that exhilarated him . . ." (p. 135). The visit was a high point in his life, as he wrote to his wife: "So this is what I had been afraid of for years!" (p. 135). In other places, he described Rome as a divine city and felt "drawn to the austere seriousness" (p. 136).

The repetition of this theme in my clinic, more than a century later, in a way that connected the oedipal contents and the attraction of the ruins of ancient Rome, was inspiring. Michael related to his father's castrating, devastating aspect, manifested mainly in his judgmental criticizing attitude, in a similar way to the inhibitions Freud felt regarding his visit to Rome. Michael also related to the reviving aspect of his father when a tangible accessibility to the historical Roman ruins was facilitated at the excavation site. It seems that in both cases, the possibility of physically visiting the site, revealing the various layers of history and pre-history, old ones beside more recent ones, was of therapeutic value. In both cases, the Rome's historic remains represented the layers of the human mind. Digging into the past, for Michael, was the connecting thread by which it was possible to establish relations with his father and his private history.

Similar to the excavation site and the Freudian conceptualization regarding the topographic model and the different levels of consciousness, the tale *The Three Feathers* presented in a previous chapter of this book, also illustrates a geologic structure, consisting of different layers. The treasures hidden beneath the surface must be hoisted above the earth to be meaningfully utilized. This is exactly how Freud defines the goals of psychoanalysis: raising the hidden, valuable unconscious material to the conscious level – a process which is often intricate and tangled.

Michael brought a photo album to one of our sessions; it contained pictures documenting the archaeological project at the dig. He held his album in the way people handle a treasured, precious piece of art, and started turning the pages, one by one, scrutinizing each photo with immense respect. A sense of holiness permeated the atmosphere during this session, probably because we were looking at Michael's inner world – the pictures of his soul. These pictures did not merely include his individual past but encompassed his being a part of a long chain of events and consisting of countless layers. These layers incorporated the present, with the two of us sitting together in my consulting room and looking at the photos, the moment in which those pictures were taken several decades earlier and the uncovering, one layer after another, of ancient Rome. For me, our sitting together echoed Freud's own history, as well as his ideas conceptualized during the early days of psychoanalysis. Leafing through the photo album, looking at the archaeological dig, helped us cope with the impressions that Michael's childhood experiences imprinted on his mental life. Talking about these impressions was not enough; we needed to view them, physically and figuratively.

Recognizing the idiomatic expression as the intersection of concrete experience and mental representation, the possibility of consolidation, in one idiom, the primary-somatic pole with the verbal-symbolic pole of mental organization (the one which enables to conceptualize experiences) may serve to echo the language of impressions used by the human psyche. In Freud's terminology, this is where the primitive coexists with the developed. To cope with Michael's resistant and prolonged symptoms, we had to pave the way to the primary levels of the mental organization.

This endeavor resembled the craft of archaeology in many respects. The analogy has been made by Freud himself, later in life, when he told Stefan Zweig: "I have made many sacrifices for my collection of Greek, Roman, and Egyptian antiquities, and actually have read more archaeology than psychology" (Gay, 1998, p. 171). To his famous patient, called by him Wolf Man, he told that "the psychoanalyst, like the archeologist in his excavations, must uncover layer after layer of the patient's psyche, before coming to the deepest, most valuable treasures" (Gay, 1998, p. 171). Gay mentions that

> Collecting antiquities was for Freud a lifelong avocation which he pursued with devotion and with system. When his old friend Emanuel Lowy, professor of archeology in Rome, and later in Vienna, was in town, he visited Freud ... but he enormously enjoyed his statuettes and fragments, the early purchases he could barely afford ... and that Freud asserted that similar to the archeologist, the psychoanalyst uses tools of his own time to reach findings that are emerging from earlier times.

Analogous to the way Freud borrowed from archeology to conceptualize the mind, in Michael's life, the concept of digging was present as both a metaphor and a distinct experience. Together they addressed his relations with his ancestors – either his own father or his ancient forebears in Rome. The concept of digging was also associated with the psychotherapeutic enterprise. Actually, Freud himself was called "the archeologist of the mind" (Gay, 1998, p. xix). The question of how we should dig, how we should expose the past, how we should touch the fragments with the most appropriate, caring attention was a core, fundamental question in our endeavor. Peter Gay describes how Freud's "antique objects gave him sheer visual and tactile pleasure; Freud caressed them with his eyes or fondled them as he sat at his desk" (p. 171). Gay writes that "Even more obscurely, his antiques seemed reminders of a lost world to which he and his people, the Jews, could trace their remote roots" ... and that "the things, he observed, put me in high spirits and speak of distant times and lands" (p. 172). In the introduction to the case study of his famous patient Dora, Freud compares the problems of "incompleteness of my analytic results" to the problems of "those discoverers whose good fortune it is to bring to the light of day after their long burial the priceless though mutilated relics of antiquity" (1963, p. 7). In both cases Freud identified the analyst as well as the archeologist as those who had to complete the missing evidence by using the existing material: "I have restored what is missing, taking the best models known to me from other analyses, but like a conscientious archaeologist I have not omitted to mention in each case where the authentic parts end and my constructions begins" (p. 7).

Michael strived to describe to me the events in the excavation site as if they were taking place at the present moments of our therapeutic meetings. He invited me to join him as he visited the halls of curiosity, to witness the fascinating process which was the landscape of his childhood. I accepted this invitation to merge the dust-covered memories, shadowed by his father, and create a place where ancient remains and fragments, older than his own history, as a way to connect deeply and tangibly with his father and his father's past.

In Freud's view, the analyst should release his patient from the dangerous illusion, and help him or her realize that what they see as they view life, in reality, is nothing but the reflection of the past. Michael had invited me into the archeological dig so that the past's reflection would emerge. Revealing the history by our shared leafing through the photo album, looking at the pictures taken at the excavation site, was not merely "digging" into the past. It was an experience taking place in the present; something that happened in my consulting room in a way that created space for past experiences, permitting a new encounter.

"Living-fossils" is a concept that represents ways of life that haven't changed for prolonged eras in evolutionary terms. To an extent, the experiences described in this book operate similarly; it is as if they were frozen in time during their efforts to create a connection with other experiences and the entire mental system. During the years in which Freud analyzed Cacilie, he assumed that traumatic experiences create a sort of structure within a structure, which he called "secondary consciousness" – a state which is detached from mental life and ordinary consciousness. After a few versions, Freud placed the detached experiences in the earliest developmental years and believed that their fixation was responsible for their detachment from mental life – as if some anachronism, preserved since the early experiences, hadn't gone through the symbolization process (Masson, 1985). This is an example of how the primitive still exists beside the more developed.

Psychoanalysis explains the existence of archaic components in mental life by using terms such as fixation, unconscious fantasy, unconscious desire, unconscious conflict, defense and so forth. However, as argued in a previous work (Raufman and Yigael, 2011), even though each of these terms constitutes an excellent contribution to the ongoing endeavor of understanding these components, none of them provides an accurate description of the phenomenon presented in this book – the experience which is embedded in language, or the language which is embedded in the experience. The challenge is not only to describe these experiences, but to identify and associate them with the exact expression which they describe in non-verbal terms, and vice versa: to identify and associate the verbal expression with the experiences that are responsible for their creation. Familiar idiomatic expressions such as "digging into the past," "the train has left the station," "below the surface," "it does not smell good" and others, have the potential to "touch" the primary somatic layers of mental organization, to evoke them and even revive them. They may be yielded by the somatic experience itself. Associated behavioral symptoms present experiences that are not difficult to describe, but it is challenging to identify and connect to the exact idioms realized by them non-verbally, and vice versa: it is extremely difficult to identify the idiomatic expression and connect it to the experiences to which it owes its existence.

Michael's ability to connect with his past from a new place, in a way that echoed primary life, was his means of escape, his egress from an imprisoning dead end. This option removed some of the dust that covered so many of his experiences, probably like the antiques buried underneath the surface, waiting for the loving hand of the archeologist to expose them to the light of day and provide them with the recognition of their existence. Returning to the idea presented at the outset of this chapter, regarding the apparently absurd intention to avoid focusing on the problem itself, but rather the healing methodology: I conclude this chapter by citing Cartwright (2013) who viewed the therapist's containing quality (Bion, 1962; 1963; 1967) as

> emerging out of a bi-personal field (Baranger and Baranger, 2008; Civitarese, 2012; Ferro, 2004) where experience is constructed by patient and therapist. The result is a fictionalized experiencing process that renders unarticulated experience bearable, thinkable and meaningful (Cartwright, 2013, p. 73). As Bion (2005) puts it: 'We may not make much progress, but . . . our thinking may strengthen our mental musculature . . . in such a way that our mental capacity would be able to carry a bigger load' (p. 75). This observation is clearly reflected in current mentalisation-based approaches, where the processes of thinking and representing experience are privileged over particular content (e.g., Bateman and Fonagy, 2004).
>
> (Cartwright, p. 91)

References

Baranger, M. and Baranger, W. (2008). The Analytic Situation as a Dynamic Field, *International Journal of Psychoanalysis*, 89(4): 795–826.
Bateman, A.W. and Fonagy, P. (2004). Mentalization-Based Treatment of BPD, *Journal of Personality Disorders*, 18(1): 36–51.
Bion, W.R. (1962). A Theory of Thinking, *International Journal of Psychoanalysis*, 43: 306–310.
Bion, W.R. (1963). *Elements of Psychoanalysis*. London: Karnac.
Bion, W.R. (1967). *Second Thoughts*. London: William Heinemann Medical Books.
Bion, W.R. (2005). *The Italian Seminars*. London: Karnac Books.
Cartwright, D. (2013). Clinical Features of the Container Function, *Psychoanalytic Psychotherapy in South Africa*, 21(2): 73–104.
Civitarese, G. (2012). *The Violence of Emotions: Bion and post-Bionian Psychoanalysis*. New York: Routledge.
Ferro, A. (2004). *Seeds of Illness, Seeds of Recovery: The Genesis of Suffering and the Role of Psychoanalysis*. London: Routledge.
Freud, S. (1930/2016). *Civilization and Its Discontent*. T. Dufresne (Ed.) and G.C. Richter (Trans.). Ontario: Broadview Press.
Freud, S. (1963). *Dora: An Analysis of a Case of Hysteria*. P. Rejf (Ed.). New York: Touchstone.
Gay, P. (1998). *Freud: A Life for Our Time*. New York and London: Norton.
Masson, J.M. (1985). *The Complete Letters of Sigmund Freud to Wilhelm Fliess, 1887–1904*. Cambridge, MA: Belknap Press.
Raufman, R. and Yigael, Y. (2011). "Feeling Good in Your Own Skin," Part II: Idiomatic Expressions: The Language's Way to Connect with the Primary Levels of Mental Organization, *American Journal of Psychoanalysis*, 71: 16–36.

Section 2

From experience to language

In the first section of this book, I discussed how certain idiomatic expressions bridge the gap between the primary psychic language and symbolic speech, as well as between concrete and abstract modes of expression. I heavily relied on Freudian ideas. Freud, at least during the early phases, focused his theory on a one-person psychology, emphasizing the drives. Later analysts, especially those espousing object relation theories, shifted the focus to the two-person psychology. In his paper "Primitive Emotional Development" (1945), Winnicott states that mother and baby (analogous to analyst and analysand) "live an experience together." Winnicott emphasized not only the importance of feeling alive as essential for development, but also the significance of being alive together, living an experience jointly. I tried to illustrate how the Freudian idea regarding the affinity between somatic symptoms and verbal expressions may not only be identified (and sometimes interpreted) in the therapeutic dialogue, but also used to attain new meanings in the context of two persons sharing the experience together. In the chapters "Below the surface" and "Digging into the past" I showed that understanding the idioms' connection to the dreams and symptoms provided new possible meanings to the drama occurring inside the psyche. In the two other chapters in the first section, "That train has left the station" and "What's the matter?" I emphasized the way I joined in the process so I could live the experiences with Danny, Shirley and Gabi. Connecting the words "meter," "matter" and "mother" could not have occurred unless a living relationship was in the process of coming into being. In addition, each of these words could attain its unique, "living" meaning only in the context of a shared experience, in which our physical bodies and presence played an active role in the scene.

The second part of this book discusses another aspect of the ongoing interchange of the two languages – how therapists use their primary, often non-verbal experiences to explore their patients' unconscious worlds. Out of this non-verbal realm, they create the appropriate verbal conceptualization so they could not only share primary experiences, but discuss them verbally.

Despite increasing knowledge in the field, a great deal is still shrouded in mystery. Dredging up essential messages from the depth of the mind, those unavailable on the surface, requires letting ourselves get lost time after time, then find our way back. Further development in psychoanalytic literature shifted the focus from binary to tertiary structures, i.e., from relations between objects and subjects to a relational matrix, focusing on co-created experiences and calling for mutual recognition.[1]

Before elaborating on the differences between object-relation theories and relational analysis, I suggest that this development in psychoanalytic literature – the move from one-person psychology to two-person psychology, and then to the more complex relational matrix – may be viewed as parallel to the development of the individual mind. It is first preoccupied with internal drives and sensations, then perceiving relationships as objects and subjects, gradually gaining the capability of identifying the characteristics of the other, and, if allowed, progress to a more developed relational matrix, in which mutual recognition unfolds – a developmental phase that is not always accomplished.

Like other processes in psychic development, as well as in psychoanalytic literature, these expansions are often tacit, tangled, subtle and intricate. Psychoanalysis is often regarded as an art, not merely due to our articulated way of alternating between words and more primary modes of expression within the therapeutic enterprise, but also due to the ongoing endeavor to theoretically conceptualize the non-verbal. I find *belles-lettres* the most fitting arena where I can touch the junction at which the verbal meets the non-verbal, and the conscious meets the unconscious. The following quote is the opening lines of a poem by the Hebrew poet Guy Perel (2013). I find it reflects the development of subjectivity emerging through the gaze of our beloved.[2] The name of the poem is *Standing in Front of Me*:

> My growing-up daughter pulls
> the final baby off me
> like a blanket in the morning.
> Daily she watches me less from inside me and already
> she stands in front of me
> recognizing my features.

The world reflected in this poem is in motion; we witness a shifting relationship, perpetually transforming, never static. She is not a grown-up daughter, but a growing-up daughter, who pulls the "baby" away from her father, like throwing off a blanket in the morning. Bursting with active verbs (growing-up, pulls off, watches, stands, recognizing) that take place in present time and go on happening, the poem reveals how the daughter's perception of her father is continually changing and in turn, altering his perception of her. No longer a part of him and his psyche, she acquires the subjectivity of her individual state. And as she sees him as a separate person and recognizes his features, he can do so as well. The poem illustrates the relational belief that the human mind is interactive rather than monadic.

Relational psychoanalysis calls this gradual process "mutual recognition." Various thinkers describe it as the persistent preoccupation with establishing and maintaining such intra-psychic and interpersonal space. They relate it to the oscillation between the connection and separation process where a baby perceives his mother as part of his own body and psyche. Only later can the baby gradually begin to recognize the mother as a separate entity, and the process continues throughout life. Intersubjective and relational approaches emphasize the function of the parent/therapist's subjectivity in this process, as well as Perel's poem. What I like about Perel's poem is how it addresses the evolving fatherly subjectivity. In recent decades, psychoanalytic literature is more and more occupied with the question of maternal subjectivity, as if taking for granted the subjectivity of the father. The poem opens a room for the father to enter and play an active role in the developing relations with his daughter instead of merely representing the pole of individuation/the symbolic or other concepts given by different schools of thought. Perel's poem illustrates how important insights regarding human psyche and development emerge from poetry, allowing the mind to speak for itself. Even though the father was an individual before his daughter came into his life, her maturing gaze reassures his own subjectivity and provides it with new meanings. Reciprocally, his capacity to grow and experience himself as a subject, and not merely an object used by his daughter, promotes the daughter's emerging subjectivity and ability to recognize her father as a separate individual.

I suggest that this sequence is parallel to the development of psychoanalytic literature. This assumption helps me in combining ideas formulated by different schools of thought in psychoanalysis and proposing intervention where early Freudian ideas are used in an inter-subjective and relational context. For that purpose, I briefly review previous conceptualizations regarding the relations between analysts and analysands. Melanie Klein (1946) and her followers show how analysts are affected and invaded by their analysands in terms of projective identification; a mechanism often activated when the patients unconsciously entrust the therapists with conflictual material that they are not yet capable of owning. The therapists, in turn, identify with this material and experience it as their own. Ogden (1979) defines projective identification as a group of fantasies and accompanying object relations intended to get rid of unwanted aspects of the self, depositing these unwanted ''parts'' into another person, and finally, recovering a modified version of what was extruded (p. 357). For example, I recall a session in which the patient, a senior officer in the army, suddenly asked me, in the middle of our conversation: "Do you hear the airplanes above? There is an upcoming war threatening to destroy our country and we are about to be bombed." While he was laconically detailing the potential dangers and how we are going to be bombed, I started imagining how I should shield myself and where I would find shelter. Withdrawing into a state of mental seclusion, where I was trying to protect myself against an unexpected invasion, I found it difficult to communicate with him; I tried to minimize my presence. Only later I realized how he entrusted his anxiety to me and hence freed himself from an overwhelming threat of a devastating bomb. In addition, by "scaring" me, he unconsciously ensured that I would not get too close to him.

My detachment could also be partly understood as caused by this unconscious mechanism, aimed at shielding myself from invasions and "bombing." However, the short conversation concealed another type of fear. Later, after I shared my feelings with him, he admitted that the first time he saw me, he found me beautiful and thought I presented a dominant, sexy presence. He did not expect a psychologist to look like that and was concerned that the potential clash of drives and feelings, which he did not wish to feel, might make it difficult to be open with me and interfere with the therapy. While having personal feelings of affection and sexual attraction for the analyst is common in psychotherapy, the play of words here was interesting. The word "bomb" ("ptzatza" in Hebrew), which was the word that crossed his mind, literally means a "bomb," but in urban slang, it describes a beautiful, sexy woman. Hebrew speakers in the 1940's adapted the word directly from the English word "bombshell" which was coined at that time in the United States. The *Urban Dictionary* describes the story:

> This term came from Rita Hayworth, the gorgeous, notorious movie star whose image was painted on the side of the first atomic bomb

exploding at the Bikini Atoll in World War II. This started the trend of calling stunning, sexy females bombshells – and the phrase is still commonly used today.
(www.urbandictionary.com/define.php?term=bombshell)

Clearly, at a certain point in that first meeting, our conversation held the peril of intimacy, so he remarked about the possibility of real bombs to warn me of the potential danger, his fear that he might fall under the charm of the "bombshell" who was analyzing him; that he might "be bombed" by me. The mechanism of projective identification is sometimes the only way by which patients can unconsciously communicate their inner situation – how they feel, what is yet to be processed, what are the difficulties with which they cope, etc. A vital tool in understanding what occurs in the therapeutic relationships is the therapist's ability to identify his or her own inner experiences such as thoughts, feelings and even somatic reactions and behaviors, as they arise in response to the patient's projected material. In recent decades, relational psychoanalysis is more emphasized. In it, therapeutic relationships are viewed as a co-created, shared experience, rather than considering the patient as the source of the problematic material. The information on this subject is too large for this introduction, but much further reading is available.[3] Thinking about the "bombing" situation, I have to admit that I could not bring this issue into consciousness as I felt threatened by the possibility of a patient falling in love with me, or being sexually attracted to me.[4] Unlike other situations described in previous chapters of this book, I preferred to avoid addressing my presence, so we were both caught in an impasse. Hence, viewing my withdrawal as responding to the difficult material emerging solely from my patient's unconscious mind would be ignoring my part and responsibility in our relations. When my patient commented that a potential bomb threatened *our* country, he reminded both of us that we shared the same fate in our therapeutic enterprise. It was a way of compelling both of us to deal with the potentially overwhelming material.

In describing the influential works of Benjamin, Mitchell and Aron (1999) note her focus on the question of how we relate to the other's independent consciences, and "how separate subjects can recognize each other as equivalent centers of experience" (p. 181). In so asserting, they emphasize

> Benjamin's ability to maintain an approach of both/and rather than of either/or. Where we all tend to collapse the tension in an argument

toward one side or the other, Benjamin has managed better than most to keep the tension, holding out for a theoretical space that makes room for complexity and paradox.

(p. 182)

In emphasizing her *ability*, we can see how psychoanalytic writing is perceived in terms of a developmental achievement; a notion that allows comparing the development of the individual to that of psychoanalytic literature. Within the creative field of playing with concepts and ideas in a way that combines a theory of thinking with object relation and intersubjective theories, it is worth noting the work of Bion and his followers, who expanded the idea of projective identification, and created a theory of thinking, based on the containing function of the parent/therapist.[5]

Perel's poem illustrates the shift from a one-directional gaze into mutual recognition. It illustrates constant switches between gazes; the reader cannot decide who is looking at whom. Is it the daughter who sees her father? Or does the father see her, and can report what he sees? Is he writing about himself and his own experience, or about her, growing up? And if he is writing about himself, this is a changing self, as his daughter's gaze is no longer located inside him. Something has been fundamentally changed, forcing us to ask: can the father describe himself, while his self is ever changing? Can he describe the focal point from which he is being looked at – his daughter – while this "point" continually shifts according to his gaze? In a way, these questions usually accompany us in our therapeutic realm, shared with our patients.

Cartwright emphasizes the passion involved in this process:

> While listening to the patient, commenting and interpreting, the therapist demonstrates a containing "presence" through inviting the patient to join a passionate inquiry into what is on both of their minds. While the analytic field is imbued with a range of emotions, it is the qualities of passion, faith and curiosity that approximate the emotional character of the containing function. This leads to the intersubjective qualities of feeling held in another's mind, seeing oneself in the other's mind, an important part of the container function.
>
> (2013, p. 97)

When describing Danny, whose chronic tardiness was partly explained as realizing the idiomatic expression "that train has left the station," I was trying to illustrate my subjective engagement in the therapeutic enterprise and my own growth and self-exploration in this process. This has been done alongside the way I used the Freudian idea of reading the affinity between somatic/behavioral symptoms and verbal expressions. Using the concept of the Social Unconscious, I illustrated how my socio-relational world was connected to Danny's, and how working with his unconscious facilitated my self-revelation and exploration. In the case description of Shirley, I illustrated our mutual exploration of each other in a way very similar to the one described in Perel's poem.

These ideas illustrate how being a psychotherapist is unlike any other profession. We accept an ongoing invitation to be in close contact with our inner world, sometimes emerging from entirely unexpected contingencies. We are willing to get lost over and over again, and then find our way from an unknown place. Our ability to face ambiguity, to allow ourselves not to know what is happening, to tolerate confusion, and then to regain a sense of "truth" is the beating heart of the therapeutic enterprise. No wonder psychoanalysis is often regarded as art.[6]

As illustrated, certain idiomatic expressions and their realization in the form of behaviors, bridge the gap between concrete and metaphoric aspects in human experience. Addressing this phenomenon in a relational view, we may ask how the realization of idiomatic expressions is connected to the developmental process of moving from a one-person psychology to binary relations, to a tertiary structure. We may raise questions regarding the function of the *Other* in this phenomenon, in which the inner (somatic) and the external (the other) perpetually interchange.

While the chapters presented in the first section mainly address the connection between somatic aspects and idiomatic expressions in the individual's psyche, the second part discusses the shared realm, co-created by the therapist and the patient. Each of the following chapters presented in this section illustrates certain aspects of the two participants living and co-creating an experience together. In this intersubjective relational process, the connections between somatic and metaphoric modes of expressions attain new meanings.

Notes

1 The literature dedicated to this matter is too myriad to be summed up here. See, for example, Mitchel and Aron 1999–2005; Bromberg 1991; Benjamin 1990; 2004; Davies 1994.
2 The poem was published in Hebrew, in Perel, Guy. (2013). *There is a Spot Above your Head*. Tel Aviv: Hakibbutz Hameuchad (Hebrew). English translation by Ilil Arbel. The poem is cited here in the permission of the poet and the Hebrew publisher.

3   This reminds us of Grotstein's definition of projective identification: a concept that focuses on both an intrapsychic experience and an interpersonal process (Grotstein, 1985). As Benjamin puts it "the idea of the paranoid-schizoid position (Klein, 1946) . . . does not address this intersubjective dynamic of the two-person relationship and its crucial manifestations at the level of procedural interaction" (Benjamin, 2004, p. 9). Symington points out the shared responsibility of both patient and analyst regarding the feelings generated during therapy, noting that the patient is often "blamed" for feelings experienced by the analyst. He suggests that: "This type of description implies that there are only two blamable objects in the room: patient and analyst. There is a third term: the process in which both are involved" (Symington, 1983, p. 288).

4   For a notable illustration regarding how to work with love and erotic transference and countertransference in a relational context, see Davies, J.M. (1994). Love in the Afternoon: A Relational Reconsideration of Desire and Dread, *Psychoanalytic Dialogues*, 4: 150–170.

5   Bion's theory of thinking is based on transforming beta elements (unmetabolized psyche/soma/affective experience) into alpha elements (thoughts that can be thought by the thinker). This is possible by the containing function of the analyst: Bion took for granted that the infant requires a mind to help it tolerate and organize experience. For Bion, thoughts exist prior to the development of an apparatus for thinking. The apparatus for thinking, the capacity to have thoughts "has to be called into existence to cope with thoughts" (1984, p. 111). Thinking, the capacity to think the already existing thoughts, develops through another mind providing alpha-function (1962, p. 83) – through the "container" role of maternal reverie.

> To learn from experience alpha-function must operate on the awareness of the emotional experience; alpha-elements are produced from the impressions of the experience; these are thus made storable and available for dream thoughts and for unconscious waking thinking . . . If there are only beta-elements, which cannot be made unconscious, there can be no repression, suppression, or learning.
>
> (Bion, 1962, p. 8)

Alpha-function works upon undigested facts, impressions and sensations, that cannot be mentalized – beta-elements. Alpha-function digests beta-elements, making them available for thought (1962, pp. 6–7). Cartwright asserts that

> Although the analytic relationship is essentially asymmetrical (the therapist is there to be receptive to the patient's experience . . .), the process of containing unarticulated emotional experience relies on the patient as colleague and collaborator (Bion, 1992). It is far from a static or one-directional process represented by the therapist doing all the mental digestion until the contained can be delivered back to the patient in the form of an interpretation. In Bion's understanding, the container-contained configuration constantly switches from therapist to patient as they struggle together to represent and contain unmetabolised experience.
>
> (Cartwright, 2013, p. 80)

Cartwright illustrates the role of the therapist's subjectivity in Bion's theory of thinking, noting that

> containing is best understood as emerging out of a bi-personal field (Baranger and Baranger 2008, Civitarese 2012; Ferro, 2004) where experience is constructed by patient and therapist. The result is a fictionalized experiencing process that renders unarticulated experience bearable, thinkable and meaningful. Crucial to the containment process is the therapist's negotiation of tensions between his role as "dream object" and "proper object" (Caper, 1999), as well as the patient's experience of various aspects of the therapist's subjective presence."
>
> (p. 73)

6 See Ogden's paper, "This Art of Psychoanalysis" (2007).

References

Baranger, M. and Baranger, W. (2008). The Analytic Situation as a Dynamic Field, *International Journal of Psychoanalysis*, 89(4): 795–826.

Benjamin, J. (1990). Recognition and Destruction: An Outline of Intersubjectivity. In: S. Mitchel and L. Aron (Eds.). *Relational Psychoanalysis*. New York and London: Routledge.

Benjamin, J. (2004). Beyond Doer and Done To: An Intersubjective View of Thirdness, *Psychoanalytic Quarterly*, 73(1): 5–46.

Bion, W.R. (1962). *Learning from Experience*. New York: Jason Aronson.

Bion, W.R. (1984). *Second Thoughts*. London: Karnac.

Bion, W.R. (1992). *Cogitations*. London: Karnac.

Caper, R. (1999). *A Mind of One's Own: A Kleinian View of Self and Object, Vol. 32*. London: Routledge.

Cartwright, D. (2013). Clinical Features of the Container Function, *Psychoanalytic Psychotherapy in South Africa*, 21(2): 73–104.

Civitarese, G. (2012). *The Violence of Emotions: Bion and Post-Bionian Psychoanalysis*. New York: Routledge.

Davies, J.M. (1994). Love in the Afternoon: A Relational Reconsideration of Desire and Dread, *Psychoanalytic Dialogues*, 4: 150–170.

Ferro, A. (2004). *Seeds of Illness, Seeds of Recovery: The Genesis of Suffering and the Role of Psychoanalysis*. London: Routledge.

Grotstein, J.S. (1985). *Splitting and Projective Identification*. New York: Jason Aronson.

Klein, M. (1946). Notes on Some Schizoid Mechanisms. In: *The Writings of Melanie Klein, Vol. 3: Envy and Gratitude and Other Works*. London: Hogarth Press, pp. 1–24.

Mitchel, S.A. and Aron, L. (Eds.). *Relational Psychoanalysis*. New York and London: Routledge.

Ogden, T.H. (1979). On Projective Identification, *International Journal of Psychoanalysis*, 60: 357–373.

Ogden, T.H. (2007). *This Art of Psychoanalysis: Dreaming Undreamt Dreams and Interrupted Cries*. New York: Routledge.

Perel, G. (2013). *There is a Spot Above your Head*. Tel Aviv: Hakibbutz Hameuchad [Hebrew].

Symington, N. (1983). The Analyst's Act of Freedom as Agent of Therapeutic Change, *International Journal of Psychoanalysis*, 10(3): 283–291.

Winnicott, D.W. (1945). Primitive Emotional Development, *International Journal of Psychoanalysis*, 26: 137–145.

Chapter 5

It does not smell good
(I smell a rat)

The issue of smell or odors in the context of the analytic endeavor can be quite challenging.

When presenting a case of a patient who had emitted excessive body odor, one of the students in my clinical seminar stated: "For me, body odor is not negotiable. It could be a reason for therapy termination." Evidently, even when we firmly believe that every aspect of the therapeutic dialogue is relevant to understanding the patient's psyche, some characteristics can be challenging to accept. Their penetration into the therapist's consciousness may be experienced so intrusively that we have to actively concentrate on the significant messages arriving from our inner, subjective world and their functions in our therapeutic relations. This chapter will discuss the potential functions of odors in human relationships, and how we employ them in psychotherapy. I will explore the connections between concrete and metaphoric aspects of human experience and the way they are voiced in idiomatic expressions that are sometimes realized in our daily life. Smells carry deep, sensorial messages that promptly influence relationships. Therefore, working with them often echoes primary experiences that invite us to learn something about the patient's inner life, which often could not be encountered otherwise; they provide us with further implicit relational knowledge.

In reviewing the developments made over the years in working with transference and countertransference, Racker refers to Freud's description of transference as a tool by which the analysand may relive the past under improved conditions and rectify pathological decisions and destinies. In addition, Racker suggests three different meanings of countertransference that may assist the analyst in his function as interpreter, since transference affects the analyst's behavior and interferes with his action as object of the patient's re-experience in that new fragment of life that is the analytic situation, in which the patient should meet with greater understanding and objectivity than he found in the reality or fantasy of his childhood.

(Racker, 2007, p. 725)

When working with physical, sensorial experiences, these ideas may carry special relevancy.

Aaron suffered from overpowering body odor. A challenging situation for me, since from the first meeting I found it extremely difficult to share a room with a patient who had come to me seeking relief from his suffering and pain. I felt trapped, and my frustration intensified when Aaron told me he needed therapy because he felt his wife didn't love him. She had had several affairs throughout their marriage and avoided having sex with him. Even before they got married, she was in love with another man, who didn't want to marry her. From the beginning of their relationship, his wife treated him as second best, a compromise that helped her recover from her rejection by the other man. Aaron accepted this "role" and was accustomed to living with a woman who had never loved him, until one day, he simply could not bear it any longer.

In addition to his body odor problem, Aaron had hearing difficulties, which made it even worse for me since I could not keep my distance from him. He repeatedly asked me to come closer to him so he could hear me better. At first, he said he only wished to "make his wife stop cheating on him," but it soon became apparent that we had to explore a more fundamental, primary experience he was accustomed to – the conviction that it was impossible to love him or be attracted to him. He unwaveringly believed that anyone who wished to get closer to him did so with ulterior motives, some form of personal gain; after all, Aaron was a very successful person in his profession and other areas of life. This basic experience attained an immediate legitimacy in the clinic, since I, his own therapist, found it extremely difficult to be with him; I only agreed to be in the same room with him because of our "professional contract." Actually, my immediate, automatic response was: "No wonder his wife feels this way. It's very difficult to be with him . . .".

The pervasive presence of the foul odor in the room allowed no repression or even sublimation of the harsh internal aspects that had accompanied Aaron throughout his life. However, it also made staying in the room almost impossible because, regardless of how the therapy progressed, I could not cultivate a sense of closeness and empathy for Aaron – feelings that are crucial to the analytic endeavor. By bringing me his worst issues, in their most tangible form, Aaron seemed to force me to experience him at his worst, as if to test me – would I stay with him in the room, or would I reject him? It seemed this was his only way of telling me a profound truth about his intimate life, to enact primary experiences by the sensorial system. However, this "method" was exceptionally problematic on both the physical and the emotional level. I couldn't help but compare our situation to his relationship with his wife; like her, I found myself occupied with thoughts of "betrayal," wishing to be elsewhere, comparing and preferring the company of my other patients, all of whom were more pleasant to be with than Aaron.

In such situations, we should examine our understanding of transference and countertransference processes. Unlike some observations formulated in the 1950's, which viewed countertransference as an obstacle which hinders understanding and interpretation, as it influences the analyst's behavior and has a decisive effect upon the patient's re-experiencing of his childhood (see, for example, Little (1951), who stresses the analyst's tendency to reenact the behavior of the patient's parents, while satisfying certain needs of his own, rather than those of the analysand), it is most common to regard countertransference as a tool with which to understand the analysand. Heimann (1950) suggested that the analyst's unconscious "understands" that of his patient. This rapport on the deep level comes to the surface in the form of feelings which the analyst notices in response to his patient, in his countertransference. The analyst's emotional response is frequently closer to the patient's true psychological state than his conscious judgment. Contemporary psychoanalysts further developed various aspects of working with countertransference, emphasizing the preverbal level on which intrapsychic and interpersonal communication takes place, as well as the need of making sense and allow the process of mentalization.

Although at that stage of the therapy I was not as yet fully aware of the possible meanings of my reactions toward Aaron, I considered the possibility that he was unconsciously using his body odor issue to convey something about his "smelly," "fishy" life as the means of ushering me into his internal world. By unconsciously letting myself identify with these projected materials, I could feel the guilt of being a woman who couldn't physically tolerate the man with whom she was sharing the same space. In addition, I could also feel the strain of bearing the physical proximity, striving for the appropriate distance, and being trapped in a relationship with no way out. Winnicott acknowledged the importance of negative feelings in the countertransference, in his *Hate in the Countertransference*

(1949), in which he refers to the "objective and justified hatred" of the analyst, while becoming the analysand's object in his re-experience of childhood. To further address Winnicott's question of whether the analyst should bear his hatred in silence or communicate it to the analysand, Little suggested admitting the analyst's countertransference to the analysand and interpreting it, not only in regard to "objective" countertransference reactions (as suggested by Winnicott), but also to "subjective" ones. However, bearing these ideas in mind does not always lead to therapeutic achievements, and the therapist must wait for the appropriate moment to communicate her reactions. I had to wait for a turning point to arrive. In retrospect I could observe that adopting the above theoretical conceptualizations (which enabled me to understand my complicated feelings of repulsion and blame toward Aaron as a response to Aaron's relational world) was my way, at that point, to ignore my own part and responsibility in our relations. More about it later.

And then it happened, and not for the first time for me. As soon as a patient and I reach the point where we feel that something simply has to change, a certain answering gesture is often shown by one of us. These unconscious processes in the minds of both patient and therapist are sometimes so intricate and delicate that it's hard to pinpoint exactly how they happen. One day, Aaron showed up for the session, carrying his regular bag in one hand, while in his other hand he held a big package of toilet paper. He casually mentioned that on his way to my clinic he had entered the nearby pharmacy to buy a package of toilet paper since he ran out of it at home. He said it nonchalantly, as if it were quite natural to show up for a session with a big package of toilet paper, and then proceeded to put the package down on the table between us, ready to begin. To hear one another, I had to bend over the enormous package of toilet paper in an attempt to get closer to him. I felt completely and uncomfortably immersed in both his foul body odor and the toilet paper, as if the highly visible toilet paper symbolized the entire situation, concretely expressing all the things that were between us: a foul smell, dirt, an object that should be gotten rid of, and something requiring . . . toilet paper. This was a moment of insight. I could, of course, simply move the package, or ask Aaron to put it somewhere else. However, at this point it was evident that the package was not only present in the room, but also served as a tool of communication, carrying an important message not only identified by the sense of smell, but seen by the eyes. There the package remained between us – both connecting and separating us. Finally, things were metaphorically and concretely "on the table." I asked Aaron how he felt, as I bent towards him, and he was angry and felt rebuked. Actually, it was the first time he had overtly expressed anger toward me, and not just talked about the hypothetic negative feelings he felt in other places and situations in his life, mostly in his relations with his wife. I decided to ask him if it was natural for him to carry a package of toilet paper around with him, and if he had ever shown up this way elsewhere. In the conversation that followed, it was possible to discuss the various associations aroused by the toilet paper, as well as the hidden declaration in bringing it to the session. (Aaron later mentioned that he could easily have bought it after the session, rather than before.)

At that point, it was finally possible to discuss the body odor issue. I couldn't admit that I found his odor highly offensive. Certain things are too fragile and hurtful, even though some analysts would disagree with me. However, what I could do was inquire whether he sometimes asked his wife to get close to him, even at times when she showed no willingness to do so, and if so, how she tended to react. I have noticed that it was easier for me to shift the blame to him and discuss his relations with his wife, instead of handling it in the here and now, but felt I could not react differently. I could not yet tolerate such an intimate dialogue. It was as if we were caught in an impasse. He replied that his wife didn't like the way he smelled. He admitted this tearfully and with great sorrow as if his wife were rejecting him at that very moment. It made me feel worse. I was thinking that actually I am the one who rejects him, by not admitting my feelings. And even though it was still verbally unspoken, this sense of rejection seemed to stand between us as we faced each other in the room. As Billow has put it:

> The basic premise of the intersubjective approach is that psychoanalytic data are mutually generated, co-determined by the organizing activities of both participants in the reciprocally interacting subjective worlds of patient and analyst (Stolorow, 1997). Hence, it is important to consider contributory subjective factors of the analyst . . .
>
> (1999, p. 442)

At that point I realized how not admitting my feelings was a way of avoiding contact with Aaron. Still, I couldn't do it. Searching for a way to address the repulsion without directly admitting my feelings, I asked if his decision to bring the toilet paper to our meeting had been entirely random and meaningless, or whether it was possible that it was related to a kind of need or wish to express something, to touch upon something deep and meaningful. Aaron listened carefully and replied that it was possible he wanted to say something, but he was not sure exactly what. I continued to pursue this direction and asked whether he had any clue or idea about possible meanings or associations related to this act. At this point I realized that even though I was not ready to openly share my experience, I became more aware of it. Towering between us, the "package" testified to the relevancy of this topic in the here-and-now of the immediate situation. Its physical presence enabled discussing things that couldn't be addressed up until that point. It was also an opportunity to approach his relationship with his wife, as well as his experience of himself in the world, from a new perspective.

Racker (1957) coined the terms concordant identification and complementary identifications, both based on the concept that the patient's internal world consists of object relations images: the patient is related to an internal figure from his or her past. The concordant identification is based on introjection and projection or, in other words, on the resonance of the exterior in the interior, on the recognition of what belongs to another as one's own ("this part of you is I") and on the equation of what is one's own with what belongs to another ("this part of me is you"). However, the processes developed in the therapeutic endeavor of Aaron may be referred to in terms of complementary identification, produced by the fact that the patient treats the analyst as an internal (projected) object and, in consequence, the analyst feels treated as such; that is, he identifies himself with this object. Racker points out that

> complementary identifications are closely connected with the destiny of concordant identifications: it seems that certain complementary identifications become intensified in accordance with the degree to which the analyst fails in the concordant identifications and rejects them. It is clear that rejection of a part or tendency in the analyst himself—his aggressiveness, for instance—may lead to a rejection of the patient's aggressiveness (whereby this concordant identification fails), and that such a situation leads to a greater complementary identification with the patient's rejecting object, toward which this aggressive impulse is directed.
>
> (1957, p. 733)

The smell predicament that was enacted and re-experienced in the therapeutic process demonstrated how I, as his therapist, not only heard but actually faced what Aaron felt he aroused in his significant others first as a young child and later as an adult. In other words, the feelings of rejection and disgust evoked in me during the therapeutic relationship made me react as if I were his wife. However, it seems there was no way around taking responsibility for my part in our relationship without shifting the blame elsewhere. As long as I avoided it, it was not only the repulsion that was re-constructed, but also the betrayal. This encounter revealed something deep about the betrayal, not only on the informative levels, but as an integral part of the scene. The palpable foul smell permeating the room aroused intense annoyance with Aaron's presence; I experienced aggressive feelings toward him, as well as guilt for disliking someone who needed me. Bromberg asserts that

> By living together in the enacted shadow of what is visible but not perceived, an opportunity is afforded to encounter what has been hidden in plain sight. If an analyst is emotionally and interpersonally alive as a partner while the different areas of a patient's developmental trauma are being relived safely but not too safely, the patient's threshold for the potential triggering of affect-dysregulation is raised at the brain level. This allows their relationship greater interpersonal spontaneity and creative self-expression that is carried by an expanded sense of selfhood into the world "out there."
>
> (2013, p. 1)

The smell in the room allowed me to understand how Aaron was experienced by his wife and other close persons, and . . . with me. The possibility of actually feeling this knowledge paved the way towards insights regarding the possible function of the smell in dealing with neglected psychic areas, related to matters of rejection and intimacy. From a relational perspective, Davies has asserted that

> all of the clinician's reactions to the patient and all of the patient's reactions to the therapist are threads in the tapestry that is woven by both participants/observers to form the relational matrix within which and through which the therapy unfolds.
>
> (1994, p. 5)

The therapeutic relationship, according to Davies,

> forms both the background and foreground (Pine, 1981) in which treatment occurs. As background, the relationship is the consistent holding environment (Winnicott, 1960a) in which the patient gradually learns

to trust, a good enough (Winnicott, 1960b) space that becomes safe enough for a patient to go on being (Winnicott, 1962) while she relives, tames, and slowly integrates the long split-off self and other representations originally splintered by traumatic experiences. As foreground, the therapeutic relationship is "where the action is." It is the arena in which abuse, neglect, and idealized salvation are re-experienced and in which therapist and patient participate in the emergence, identification, and working through of powerful, often chaotic, transference and countertransference paradigms. It is within the relational matrix that state-dependent traumatic memories are triggered off by aspects of transference–countertransference reenactment.

(1994, p. 5)

It was within this intricate interplay between external and internal realities that my relations with Aaron unfolded. I was caught in a dilemma whether and how to share my experience with him.

However, the smell carried additional meanings: Aaron was suspicious of the people around him. He thought they wanted to be with him not because they liked him, but because they needed something from him; he was always worried about being exploited by others. Living so long with a woman who didn't love him and wasn't attracted to him, he always mistrusted her motives and interests. Was she living with him merely because he supported her financially, or perhaps to get over another man? As a person who envisioned himself as someone who could never be loved by another, Aaron's basic encounter with the world consisted of permanent, dubious bargaining and negotiations, in which he had to be alert so as not to be taken advantage of by others.

In Hebrew, Aaron's native language, the common idiomatic expression "it does not smell good" is also associated with suspicion (in English we say "I smell a rat"). Something about Aaron's relationship with his wife, as well as our therapeutic encounter, "didn't smell good." We shared this experience in my clinic in a way that couldn't be ignored. In a previous chapter of this book, I related to how idiomatic expressions and, more specifically, expressions that include body terminologies, are the crossroads where the somatic aspect of experience meets the verbal. The idiomatic expression "something does not smell good," which echoes primary sensorial experiences, is a good example of this idea. Studies dedicated to idiomatic expressions emphasize the universal aspect of this phenomenon, even though it is apparently associated with language, and therefore with culture.

As presented in previous works (Raufman and Yigael, 2011), Freud assumes a shared origin for the most primary level of sensations and somatic idioms. It seemed as Aaron's body odor communicated a deep, primary experience. Connecting this somatic experience to the idiomatic expression "it does not smell good" ("I smell a rat") helps understanding the difficulty to be with him in terms of the suspicious nature of his relational world. To illustrate the multiple implications and examples of the affinity between idiomatic expressions and somatic sensations, I am using Darwin's observations regarding the emotions as supporting Freud's assumption, since Darwin doesn't make a clear distinction between emotions and somatic sensations (Darwin, 1952). Darwin used idiomatic expressions in his attempts to describe the expressive emotions. Not offering any explanation for using these idioms, he was satisfied with merely pointing out the linkage between expressive emotions and certain verbal expressions. This is an opposite process from the one I suggest in describing Aaron's therapeutic process – deciphering the idiomatic expression hidden behind a behavioral symptom to provide it with metaphorical meaning.

However, as argued in a previous work (Raufman and Yigael, 2011), Darwin's observation is not merely an arbitrary reference, but a direct glimpse into the unique affinity between the level of somatic sensation and verbal expressions – especially idioms that include body parts, or physical/behavioral gestures.[1] Years later, Freud formulated the same idea, stating that experiencing the feeling of "a stab in the heart" or "a slap in the face" revives the sensation to which the linguistic expression owes its origin (Bruer and Freud, 1895, p. 254).

Almost a century later, Čermák (1988) emphasized the universality of idiomatic expressions associated with body parts. Since unlike many characteristics and aspects of life, the body is more or less similar in all cultures, it is possible to recognize how body parts function likewise in the idiomatic expressions of diverse languages. In the context of Aaron's therapy, it is worth noting Čermák's relation to the nose, which plays the same role in various cultures: it is physically associated with the sense of smell, and metaphorically detects potential dangers. The sense of smell is a basic sense among numerous animal species, and is identified with the ability to differentiate between good, healthy food, and bad, harmful food. It is also associated with one's ability to defend oneself and identify potential enemies.

. . . So, I hope I do not use the above consideration merely as an intellectualization, serving to defend my reaction to overwhelming repulsion. Instead, I wish to play with the intricate interchanges between the somatic and the symbolic/verbal, to allow a better coping mechanism when dealing with overwhelming physical experiences. The smell experience in Aaron's psychotherapeutic process helped attain profound insights related to possible motives and sources about how he tested the options of being with another. This examination occurred most concretely – by questioning his ability to share his life with another, and more specifically, a woman. However, this was not the only important issue. The assessment exposed his doubt of being worthy and deserving of love. Could he be loved at all? And could he rely on another person, and expect a woman to share a decent, rewarding life with him, without always suspecting her of ulterior motives? If it were possible, then by taking a chance on love, could he share a room with another, discuss intimate subjects, including physical issues, receive feedback and together create a pleasant, safe atmosphere?

In one session, Aaron talked more directly about his feelings of not being loved. It was the first time that he was willing to discuss this issue as associated with early childhood memories and experiences in which he did not feel secure enough in his relations with his parents. In response, I asked him if he sometimes wonders about my relation to him. Since it seemed that he was ready to have this conversation with me, I decided to share that I found it difficult to bend over the package of toilet paper in my attempt to get closer to him. "On the other hand," I continued, "maybe it was your way to make me come closer. You were right – I was a bit distant." After a pause, Aaron said that yes, now he could impart that he felt the distance between us. I answered that I am glad he could talk about it with me, and suggested that next time, when he wanted to bring something to our session, it does not have to be toilet paper. It could, instead, be something that "smelled better"; a perfume, for instance. In response, he said: "O.K., I get your point." It was the first time that we laughed together. I commented that sometimes we do things that keep people away from us, even if we want closeness. Perhaps it is not easy to trust people.

From the moment we achieved these insights, we could start to reflect on methods Aaron would develop for coping with his predicament, and start leading a life that would include intimate, trusting relationships. Aaron came to "own" his smell, that is, take responsibility and change his self-presentation. It is possible that my open and honest sharing, my willingness to overcome the difficulties of admitting my feelings, was a trust-building stage in our relationship. It was only after I earned Aaron's trust, that our relations could "smell better." In Billow's words:

Therapy at the symbiotic relational level depends on a trust that the therapist earns by establishing a balance between accommodation to and interpretation of symbiotic communications . . . interventions must be delivered and experienced benevolently, their essential purpose being to establish "a sense of contact" with an area of the projector's personality that has insufficiently mastered self-containment. Patience, timing, and tact are particularly important in establishing and maintaining emotional contact on this relational level.

(2003, p. 39)

In our therapeutic relationship, both of us became more and more open and sharing. I felt much more free and liberated in his presence and started to look forward to our meetings, without betraying him by thinking of other patients.

In an essay written in 1983 about what he called "an act of freedom," Symington wrote:

From the moment that patient and analyst engage in what we call an analysis the two are together part of an illusory system. Both are caught into it. . . . The analyst is lassoed into the patient's illusory world. . . . As the analytical work proceeds the analyst slowly disengages himself from it. In this way transference and countertransference are two parts of a single system; together they form a unity. They are the shared illusions which the work of analysis slowly undoes.

(p. 286)

The therapist's freedom, according to Symington, is limited by the analysand's projections, with which the therapist unconsciously identifies and cooperates. Being unable to tolerate my own patient's body odor evoked in me intense feelings of discomfort, making it impossible to carry on with the analytic endeavor. Instead, the therapy sessions became pregnant with guilt and the need for detachment, analogous to other relations in Aaron's life. It exhibited an example of Symington's idea of the therapist who acts, feels and thinks according to the patient's unconscious inner life. As long as the therapist is fully identified with the projected material, he is caught by a lasso and is not capable of consciously facing and dealing with the projected material. The analyst's ability to disengage himself from the lasso was referred to by Symington, as "an act of freedom," which triggers a therapeutic shift in the patient: "At the moment of insight, expressed in interpretation, the illusions or false ideas are banished both in analyst and in patient" (p. 290). However, the act of freedom cannot be originated operatively, nor can it be initiated by outside influence. The therapist has to wait for the right moment, when an internal shift in the patient's psyche occurs.

My experience with Aaron reminded me how important it is to constantly wonder and ask what was happening in our relationship, including my own sensorial experiences. This is a two-faceted position, as relevant information regarding my patients' relational world is revealed in a way that both patient and therapist experience in its primary unconscious. Only later the process of conceptualization is possible. Furthermore, the choice of not discussing the countertransference was addressed from different angles in relational psychoanalysis, pointing that in extremely regressive self-states words do not function as the means of communication. Speaking about the unobtrusive analyst, Grossmark examines cases (especially in working with patients with much envy, hatred and extreme vulnerability) in which

> addressing the patient–analyst interaction in the here-and-now is not the only way that a relational analyst works ... There are other aspects of contemporary relational treatment that reach and allow for the emergence of different registers of the patient's experiences.
> (Grossmark, 2012, p. 630)

Grossmark highlights the importance of not conflating silence, quittance and patience with neutrality, usually applied in one-person psychology. He takes from Balint (1968) and his wife Enid Balint (1993) who emphasized that in working with patients like this, the only value of the treatment

> ... has to be experienced as coming from them, from their minds, their words, and their efforts. This approach need not diverge from the sensibility that experience in the treatment is co-constructed. It does, however, allow the space for these patients to use the co-constructed "field" of treatment in the way that they need to, in the moment.
> (Grossmark, 2012, p. 632)

Grossmark reminds us that discussing the ongoing interaction in the here-and-now is not always a good idea, especially if done without considering how working in this way may affect the patient whose facility in this area is not as well developed as the analyst's. He touches upon the dilemma, also recognized by Balint, of how to work with certain regressive self-states. Whereas it has been found valuable to allow the patient experience a two-person relationship not expressed in words, later on, when the patient has emerged from the regressive, non-verbal phase, the process and the acting out can be worked through. Grossmark also takes from Bromberg (2006) and D.B. Stern (2004), to argue that "nowadays we might say that when the dissociative structure is recognized, then we can experience and talk about conflict with the patient" (Grossmark, 2012, p. 632).

The therapist's connection to her or his subjective experiences, as well as the ability to actually use them, should be handled with caution, sensitivity and accuracy, so that the so-called "objective" information regarding the patient's world would be helpful. When it comes to body odor issues, the subjects of mirroring and interpretation are delicate and complex to such an extent that it may be tempting to avoid them altogether, to prevent the possibility of considerable harm or insult. At the same time, if been verbally interpreted too early, words are at the risk of being "lifeless, repetitive and stereotyped, they don't mean what they say" (Balint, 1968, p. 177). In retrospect, I wonder if my initial avoidance of sharing my feelings with Aaron was only because I wanted to refrain from insulting him. Rather, it is possible that I wanted to ascertain that I distanced myself from the "smelly" relationship and remained "clean." Therefore, what apparently aimed to protect him, might have resulted not only in detachment but of deprivation from helpful feedback and insight. This could serve as an example of how, in certain difficult situations, we might use theory in a somewhat cynical way. In this context, it is worth quoting Gill, who suggested that the techniques of "classically" passive analyst may be iatroginic, stimulating legitimate feelings of deprivation and paranoia, and becomes an object of vigilance (Gill, 1994).

In discussing relational variations of the Bionian concepts of "container-contained," Billow describes a case in which he supervised an analyst, as they worked together to understand both her patients and the supervision relationship. He addressed the importance of owning "badness" on the part of the analyst:

> In freezing up her not-nice emotions, the analyst had attempted to suppress and deny her sense of internal badness, that is, her own bad feelings, fantasies, and thoughts, and the possibility of her bad behavior. By inviting a dialogue, and not freezing these aspects of her subjectivity, she offered us emotional ideas . . . our relationships existed as a shared, dynamic structure, growing in emotional flexibility and

abstraction, while remaining linked to our ongoing, lived-out present, and was thus commensal.

(Billow, 2003, p. 34)

Billow further suggests that

> ... to maintain commensal relations, the clinician must be in, and not above, the fray. Containing – putting into words transformations of the patient's conflictual feelings, thoughts, and fantasies – brings to the fore aspects of the history and current state of the analyst's own conflicts

and that

> ... commensally based relations are characterized by this important dimension of self-analysis, a willingness to feel, think about, and if appropriate, put into the dialogue, that which otherwise would not be shared openly, but suppressed or acted-out. Often, relational difficulties ascribed to a patient, or group, may reside in the personality of the therapist. Such techniques of silence, waiting for the patient's or group's readiness, benevolent "holding," developmentally "upward" interpretations, may be prompted by therapist-inspired dynamics of reaction formation and avoidance of the personally primitive and "not nice."
>
> (p. 35)

Ehrenberg coined the concept "intimate edge" to conceptualize how the therapeutic relationship can be used to facilitate maximum growth. By "intimate edge" she meant "that point of maximum and acknowledged contact at any given moment in a relationship without fusion, without violation" (1974, p. 424). Pointing to the importance of focusing on the space between therapist and patient, rather than the two individual participants or their separate fantasies, Ehrenberg mentions Levenson, who had remarked that

> if the therapist uses himself as an instrument, examining his own anxieties about what the patient calls out in him, and presents these to the patient, he demonstrates most directly what it feels like to be engaged in the patient's world. If the analyst is willing to be open about his own reactions these can be therapeutically useful in that they provide validation of the patient's impact, and serve to clarify exactly what this impact is.
>
> (Levenson, 1972, in Ehrenberg, p. 426)

Ehrenberg further suggests that

> openness on the part of the analyst encourages the patient to deal with his reactions to the analyst's reactions explicitly, and to validate his own experience, as well as to draw his own conclusions in this regard. If the analyst openly acknowledges the limits of his capacities he generates a more intimate encounter so that studying explicitly the patient's reactions to the analyst's limitations is possible. As the patient is confronted with the analyst's fallibility he is also confronted with necessity for his own thoughtful participation in the analytic endeavor, which is also useful. At the same time this helps focus the common human dilemmas instead of leaving the patient with some vague sense that the analyst has reached some superior state of being that he, the patient, can never attain.
>
> (p. 426)

Writing this chapter made me realize that what is most difficult for us as therapists may have the greatest curative potential. However, it is easier to accept it in retrospect. What complicated matters in Aaron's therapy consisted of relational challenges – facing, admitting and sometimes sharing my feelings – as well as linguistic issues, such as finding the words for such primary experiences. Deciphering the meaning of the words emerging from the unspeakable sensorial experience created by the presence of the odor in the room was an intermediate area between that which may be uttered and that which may not. The dilemma of whether or not to share my experience was not only a matter of avoiding insult to my patient. It was also a matter of putting into words an experience which is sensorial in its nature. However, deciphering the idiomatic expression hidden behind the sensorial experience fostered the understanding of the implicit relational knowledge regarding Aaron.

I believe that a complete avoidance of sharing any of the difficulties of our being together would have risked fixating the state of detachment, so familiar to Aaron in his private life. Also, it would have created a gulf in our relations and would, on my part, have been perceived as a lack of honesty by way of avoidance. Connecting the powerful, negative body odor to other, less embarrassing, experiences, (though not less difficult to deal with) helped bring forth the deep feelings of suspicion, repulsion and rejection to the verbal discourse. At the same time, the words "it doesn't smell good" – lurking behind the sensorial experience – might also have helped penetrate into a deep, primary area, so that our being together in the room allowed for the possible evolution of different ways of future communication between Aaron and others. Grossmark relates to severely regressed situations, quoting Balint who asserted that the analyst has to accept this and "abandon any attempt at organizing the material produced by the patient . . . the analyst must create an environment, a climate, in which he and his patient can tolerate the regression in a mutual experience" (Balint, 1968, p. 177, in Grossmark, 2012, p. 633).

In this image, Grossmark then suggests,

> psychoanalytic technique involves a sensitivity to the needs of the patient, such that these regressed parts, or self-states, can find their expression. One needs to be mindful to not be too distant, which can be experienced as abandoning, or too close, which can be experienced as encumbering and intrusive. This is a "mutuality," which is governed by sensitivities to the patient's most intimate and complex needs.
>
> (2012, p. 633)

I suggest that a deeper understanding of the phenomenon of realization of idiomatic expressions (especially somatic idioms, associated with the most intimate experiences) and its functions in the therapeutic relations, provides us with additional ways of moving between the verbal and the non-verbal and hence helps expanding the transitional area we share with our patients. In the case of Aaron, whose feelings of rejection were so deeply rooted in his relational world, my capacity to recognize the repulsive elements in a curious manner, attempting to connect the primary elements to other, "higher" aspects of his life, was of special importance.

Notes

1 Take, for example, the idiom "gnashing of teeth" as an expression which is associated with a bodily response to pain, or extreme effort. Darwin believes the origin of this idiom comes from the behavior of certain animals:

> When animals suffer from an agony of pain, they generally writhe about with frightful contortions . . . With man the mouth may be closely compressed, or more commonly the lips are retracted, with the teeth clenched or ground together. There is said to be "gnashing of teeth" in hell; and I have plainly heard the grinding of the molar teeth of a cow which was suffering acutely from inflammation of the bowels. The female hippopotamus in the Zoological Gardens, when she produced her young, suffered greatly; she incessantly walked about, or rolled on her sides, opening and closing her jaws, and clattering her teeth together.
>
> (Darwin, 1952, pp. 69–70)

While the expression "gnashing of teeth" was initially connected to painful situations, as Darwin pointed out, in daily life its meaning had been extended to include general difficult and stressful situations. Therefore, the somatic idiom "gnashing of teeth" includes the sensory nucleus of pain, expressed in the corporeal response of the gnashing of teeth, and an extended mental meaning, relating to difficult, stressful situations in general.

Darwin's project presents many other examples. He believes that the expression "lifting one's eyebrow" originated from the response to unpleasant situations such as surprise, dismay, shock and astonishment. "The eyes stare wildly as in horrified astonishment, or the brows are heavily contracted" (p. 70). He mentions that the original aim of these responses is not to communicate with the environment, but to gain relief. The expression "see red" originated from the body's response to situations that cause rage: "The face reddens, or it becomes purple from the impeded return of the blood ..." (p. 74).

These, and many other examples given by Darwin may seem fairly obvious, but they haven't yet been formally conceptualized as reflecting the affinity between verbal expressions and the primary level of physical sensations, which entails nothing more than a simple description of a given situation. These examples clearly testify to the notion that somatic expressions were created or developed out of bodily gestures and facial expressions, as well as internal somatic responses, such as "gut feeling," "feeling good in one's own skin," "a heavy heart," "difficult to stomach," "get (something) out of one's system" and "a bundle of nerves." They beautifully demonstrate Darwin's idea that when experiencing threatening situations, the entire body enters into a state of stress; the body is constricted and the nervous systems is excited: "All these signs are probably, to a large extent, and some appear to be wholly due, to the direct action of the excited sensorium" (p. 74). As to the idiom "turning a blind eye," we may see its origin in Darwin's observation that "the firm closing of the eyelids and consequent compression of the eyeball ... serves to protect the eyes from becoming too much gorged with blood" (p. 147). This response of protecting the eye from undesirable events was expanded to include other undesirable situations in life, not necessarily related to vision, as when someone turns a blind eye to protect himself from something which he finds too disturbing. Darwin's use of idioms to describe somatic responses to sensations may hint at the shared sensory origin of both somatic responses and idioms.

References

Balint, E. (1993). *Before I Was I: Psychoanalysis and the Imagination*. London: Guilford.

Balint, M. (1968). *The Basic Fault*. London: Tavistock.

Billow, R. (1999). An Intersubjective Approach to Entitlement, *The Psychoanalytic Quarterly*, 68: 441–461.

Billow, R. (2003). Relational Variations of The "Container-Contained," *Contemporary Psychoanalysis*, 39(1): 27–50.

Breuer, J. and Freud, S. (1895). Studies on Hysteria. In: J. Strachey (Ed. and Trans.) (1957), *The Standard Edition of the Complete Psychological Works of Sigmund Freud*, Vol. 2. London: Hogarth Press.

Bromberg, P.M. (2006). *Awakening the Dreamer: Clinical Journeys*. Mahwah, NJ: The Analytic Press.

Bromberg, P.M. (2013). Hidden in Plain Sight: Thoughts on Imagination and the Lived Unconscious, *Psychoanalytic Dialogues*, 23: 1–14.

Čermák, F. (1982). *Idiomatika a frazeologie češtiny*. Praha: Univerzita Karlova.

Čermák, F. (1988). On the Substance of Idioms, *Folia Linguistica*, 22(3–4): 413–438.

Čermák, F. (1994). Idiomatics. In: P. A. Luelsdorff (Ed.). *The Prague School of Structural and Functional Linguistics*. Amsterdam: John Benjamins, pp. 185–196.

Darwin, C. (1952). *The Expression of the Emotion in Man and Animals*. Chicago, IL and London: University of Chicago Press.

Davies, J.M. (1994). *Treating the Adult Survivor of Childhood Sexual Abuse*. New York: Basic Books.

Ehrenbeg, D.B. (1974). The Intimate Edge in Therapeutic Relatedness, *Contemporary Psychoanalysis*, 10: 423–437.

Gill, M.M. (1994). *Psychoanalysis in Transition: A Personal View*. Hillsdale, NJ: Analytic Press.

Grossmark, R. (2012). The Unobtrusive Relational Analyst, *Psychoanalytic Dialogues*, 22: 629–646.

Heimann, P. (1950). On Countertransference, *International Journal of Psychoanalytic Psychotherapy*, 31: 81–84.

Levenson, E.A. (1972). *The Fallacy of Understanding*. New York: Basic Books.

Little, M. (1951). Countertransference and the Patient's Response To It, *International Journal of Psychoanalytic Psychotherapy*, 16: 32–40.

Racker, H. (1957). The Meaning and Uses of Countertransference, *Psychoanalytic Quarterly*, 26: 303–357.

Racker, H. (2007). The Meanings and Uses of Countertransference, *Psychoanalytic Quarterly*, 76: 725–777.

Raufman, R. and Yigael, Y. (2011). "Feeling Good in Your Own Skin," Part II: Idiomatic Expressions: The Language's Way to Connect with the Primary Levels of Mental Organization, *American Journal of Psychoanalysis*, 71: 16–36.

Stern, D.B. (2004). The Eye Sees Itself: Dissociation, Enactment, and Understanding, *Contemporary Psychoanalysis*, 40: 197–237.

Symington, N. (1983). The Analyst's Act of Freedom as Agent of Therapeutic Change, The *International Journal of Psychoanalysis*, 10(3): 283–291.

Winnicott, D.W. (1949). Hate in the Countertransference, *International Journal of Psychoanalytic Psychotherapy*, 30: 69–74.

Chapter 6

A dancer who does not dance

> We know what we are, but know not what we may be.
> William Shakespeare, Hamlet

Some time ago I received a telephone call from a soft-spoken woman who wanted to begin therapy. I recall that listening to her velvety, caressing voice, I thought, "She sounds perfectly healthy." What did I mean by healthy? Had something already begun to happen, prior to our first meeting, that had prompted me to act like a new mother-to-be, dreaming of her future child?

When the time came for our meeting, I was sitting in my clinic, imagining what the woman with the soft voice would be like. I will call her Lillie. A young woman entered the room, immediately filling the atmosphere with words, facial expressions and fluid gestures, most of which exhibited unhappiness. She sought therapy because of general malaise. Lillie was married, childless, loved her husband, but unaccountably, was not happy. Describing her childhood, she said her family was kind and supportive, but nevertheless, she had never felt connected to her own life. She had been a good, obedient child, did not cause too much trouble and exhibited a significant talent for dancing. Growing up, she danced in diverse venues and had eventually been accepted to one of the best and most famous ensembles in the country. Promptly, however, she quit and started working as a clerk in a printing firm. She could not explain the choice of her new employment, nor why she had stopped dancing. On the one hand, she missed dancing profoundly. On the other hand, she could not bring herself to return to the world of dance. She was trapped.

I realized that here, on the couch in front of me, sat a dancer who did not dance. How was that possible? Can a singer not sing, a doctor not heal? Such an oxymoron poses the question of what describes us as human beings.

How do we identify ourselves? Is it the external status or the description that emerges from within, from our desire to do something, be something? It was clear that we were dealing with Lillie's sense of impossibility, futility and lack of self-fulfillment – the gap between potential and actual life and achievements.

What is it that makes people deprive themselves of living their life vividly and wholly? Winnicott suggests:

> It is creative apperception more than anything else that makes the individual feel that life is worth living. Contrasted with this is a relationship to external reality which is one of compliance, the world and its details being recognized but only as something to be fitted in with or demanding adaptation. Compliance carries with it a sense of futility for the individual and is associated with the idea that nothing matters and that life is not worth living. In a tantalizing way many individuals have experienced just enough of creative living to recognize that for most of their time they are living uncreatively, as if caught up in the creativity of someone else, or of a machine.
>
> (1971, p. 65)

In contrast to the emphasis in orthodox psychoanalysis upon generating insight into unconscious processes and focusing on drives, Winnicott concentrates on the importance of a familial holding environment. The difference between the two alternatives – living creatively or uncreatively – lies in the quality and quantity of environmental conditions in early life. An adequate environment facilitates the impression that the world is a place worth living in. It enables the initial provision of the primary illusion of having created the world. It also allows the illusion that what the infant creates really exists. This perspective helps link the "non-dancing" dancer with the compliant girl Lillie used to be, lacking the capacity for being – the ability to feel genuinely alive inside, which Winnicott views as essential to the maintenance of an authentic self.

Which vehicles do we have at our disposal to cope with the sense of life's expropriation? What can we do to help a patient like Lillie regain her creativity and the sense that she is actively living her own life? According to some object relation theories, as well as inter-subjective and relational approaches, the therapist's subjective, living presence in the therapeutic dialogue is at the heart of achieving this goal. Winnicott describes the treatment of a successful, middle aged family man. During a session, the patient began talking about penis envy, which struck Winnicott as odd, since the term penis envy is not usually used by men. This case clearly demonstrates the art of working with subjective emotional reactions and the intricate relations between internal and external realities. To ascribe penis envy to a man, we have to courageously stray from the apparently "objective," or "formal knowledge" that a man does not experience penis envy. We have to allow ourselves to join his inner subjective reality. Winnicott realized that he had heard this man's confession as if it were not told by a male, but by a female.

Winnicott explains:

> The change that belongs to this particular phase is shown in the way I handled this. On this particular occasion I said to him: 'I am listening to a girl. I know perfectly well that you are a man but I am listening to a girl, and I am talking to a girl. I am telling this girl: "You are talking about penis envy."
>
> (1971, p. 72)

Winnicott emphasized that this had nothing to do with homosexuality; his interpretation in each of its two parts could be thought of as related to playing, and entirely as far as possible removed from authoritative interpretation, which is very close to indoctrination. It appears that the positive trajectory shift that had occurred soon after was associated with the therapist's capacity for play-acting, the ability to be in an "as-if" zone. Winnicott continues: "After a pause the patient said: 'If I were to tell someone about this girl I would be called mad'." Taking his interpretation one step further, Winnicott surprised himself by saying: "It was not that you told this to anyone; it is I who see the girl and hear a girl talking, when actually there is a man on my couch. The mad person is myself" (pp. 72–73). The patient replied that he now felt sane – in a mad environment – and that he had been released from a dilemma. As he subsequently said: "I myself could never say (knowing myself to be a man) 'I am a girl'. I am not mad in that way. But you said it, and you have spoken to both parts of me" (p. 73). This statement shows how maneuvering between the demands posed by reality and those posed by our inner life can never go unchallenged. Over-adjustment to "objective" reality may result in a sense of uncreative compliance. Over-commitment to inner needs, drives, desires – those convincing us that the world is a place of our own creation – may lead to psychotic, chaotic states. A central aim of the psychoanalytic endeavor is to enable the inner, ostensibly "insane" speech and afford it space where one can survive without going mad. The patient knew he was a man – he never doubted it for a moment – but after Winnicott owned the madness, the patient was able to see himself as a girl from the therapist's position.

I would like to present Winnicott's description in more detail, as I later use it to discuss situations in which the therapist "dreams," or fantasizes the patient from the patient's parent's point of view. It was the very situation in which I found myself, automatically and unconsciously, from the first moment I heard Lillie's voice over the phone.

Winnicott concludes that living through a profound, personal experience was essential for arriving at the understanding he had reached.

> This complex state of affairs has a special reality for this man because he and I have been driven to the conclusion . . . that his mother . . . saw a girl baby when she saw him as a baby before she came round to thinking of him as a boy. In other words this man had to fit into her idea that her baby would be and was a girl . . . We have very good evidence from inside the analysis that in her early management of him the mother held him and dealt with him in all sorts of physical ways as if she failed to see him as a male. On the basis of this pattern he later arranged his defenses, but it was the mother's "madness" that saw a girl where there was a boy, and this was brought right into the present by my having said "It is I who am mad."
>
> (p. 73)

This example is built on delusional transference, choosing an interpretation which Winnicott admitted he nearly did not allow himself to make. Such interpretation attempts to bind early childhood experiences with present stresses, using a theoretical premise to acknowledge the importance of responses emerging from the infant's earliest environment. However, to reach this insight on a level that goes beyond intellectualization and is capable of grasping the truth, a great deal of creativity was required on the part of the therapist, including the willingness to "go mad." The readiness to delve into the experience with the patient, to live an experience together, enabled the therapist to listen to this man as if he were a girl, and only later to consider the situation causatively. The therapist dared to be submerged in delusions in a free-floating associative manner, and still maintain a connection to external reality. This is a form of in-between state – alternating between the internal and external realities of both the analyst and the analysand – a state of objective subjectivity. This phrase emphasizes the importance of subjective perception, and the therapist's awareness of the effect of the therapeutic process on himself, to enable him to reach the patient's inner reality, potentially inaccessible otherwise. In the spirit of independent analysis in the British Society (see Parsons, 2009), the analyst may serve as an analytic object to be made use of by the patient. In relational terms, Grossmark's description of the unobtrusive analyst is relevant: "... in being unobtrusive, the analyst is not neutral or abstinent, but deeply engaged and becomes the analyst the patient needs" (Grossmark, 2012, p. 629). The analyst is thus connected to both the external reality (taking into consideration someone else's needs) and the internal one (working through the therapist's own subjectivity and harnessing it for the patient's benefit).

Let us return to Lillie, the dancer who did not dance. The sound of her voice on the phone before our meeting, and her presence in my clinic, displayed gaps that had attracted my attention. While listening to her sad, heart rending story, I allowed myself to waver between the happiness in her voice, and the sadness of her body, as I witnessed her contradictory, multiple self-states (Bromberg, 1998; Davies, 2004; Mitchell, 1993). My mind became increasingly occupied with the image of Lillie dancing. The image was insistent, as if some hidden matter was crying out for recognition. I felt that this vision had never been dreamt or imagined before by anyone; I was compelled to dream about Lillie and her dancing, unwittingly entering a virgin land while not knowing how or why. This vague feeling had yet to undergo mentallization, and in retrospect, I wonder from whose imagination this image had sprung. Is it possible to imagine things that are entirely remote from our own experience?

What people undergo during early childhood or infancy is mostly out of our reach. Usually they cannot remember it, and only infrequent, vague and remote echoes of this period reverberate in our daily lives. Other relatives' reports are sometimes the only source of information available, and these reports are usually biased, as these people were part of the scene. Lacking objective sources of information, and relying on the idea that the patterns and dynamics characterizing the person would emerge in various ways throughout the therapeutic endeavor, I surrendered myself to the multiple unconscious messages Lillie and I shared. At times I see-sawed, alternately experiencing the sad, submissive, paralyzed woman, and the happy, free, liberated one – two opposing images that did not harmonize. The dual presence of voice and external appearance continuously alternated before my eyes, as if two women sat on the couch: the chained and paralyzed woman and the liberated dancer; the woman who had experienced her limitations on the physical plane; and the woman she could become, a person Lillie had yet to recognize. At those moments I felt I was creating her, not only through my own creativity, but by using the hidden potential that existed in her, yet to be born. In a paper dedicated to imagination in relational psychotherapy, Bromberg points to the overlap between the relative presence of imagination, and the relative capacity for intersubjectivity that exists in any relationship. He discusses the creative potential of the therapist's liberation of imagination (Bromberg 2013, pp. 1–14). In this associative, perhaps even delusional, mode, and for reasons I cannot rationally explain, an unbidden question arose in my mind; I asked Lillie if her mother had been a dancer as well. After a pause, she said her mother could not dance at all, as she had suffered from polio as a child. Her mother used to tell her that she had feared she would not be able to raise a child because of her limited mobility. She was constantly afraid she would drop the baby, and be unable to hold her or provide a safe environment for her development. Lillie added: "I never thought about it; I am a dancer, but my mother had polio."

We cannot know the possible desires, fears, wishes and other emotional responses Lillie had undergone while being raised by a disabled mother. We can conjecture that this mother might have experienced her daughter's mobility differently than a mother who could move freely. We can also surmise that she had to let her daughter spread her wings in a way that the mother could neither do nor even imagine. In other words, Lillie's mother was obliged to take part in a journey which she could not join in. Therefore, what crossed my mind as I saw the woman sitting across from me dancing and moving freely, probably was not imagined so tangibly by the mother, or by anyone else. I was the one who had to dream about her, imagine her and her mobility. It resulted in back-and-forth movements – as Lillie's frozen presence repeatedly transformed into the opposite image – that of a happy, dancing and vivacious woman. These two contradicting images were always split, however, and never owned by the same person at the same time. Sometimes, an impactful, compelling vision of Lillie's dancing persona took over. On other occasions, it was hard to even imagine the option of dancing since Lillie's "paralysis" was so extreme.

Every baby is usually imagined, consciously or unconsciously, before being born. Parents tend to envision their children growing up, "dreaming" them long before parenthood becomes a reality. How we view the choice of childlessness has changed in recent decades, but our descendants, future generations and those we leave behind are still deeply rooted in human experience. And even though imagination can spread its wings, rise far above reality and create new worlds, it still draws inspiration from daily experience; fantasy and reality can never be completely detached from one another. Could a woman who had suffered from polio dream motion and dancing for her baby girl? Which references would she draw upon to fantasize the way her imagined daughter would fill her space with graceful movements? Indeed, it seems as if this vision did exist and just waited for someone to dream it. Cartwright (2013) suggests that

> as part of the therapeutic process, the analyst listens using free-floating attention and reverie so as to use his own waking dream-thoughts to help the patient process emotional experience. In this sense the analyst helps the patient dream undreamt or unfinished dreams.
> (Cartwright, p. 80, referring to Ogden, 2007)

Cartwright came up with the idea of the therapist's role as "dream object," and idea refers to the therapist capacity

> to remain receptive to his dream-thoughts and reveries, welcoming them as meaningful commentaries on an emotional scene. This is not achieved in a contrived way; it emerges in my experience as I focus my attention on his experience. This process is recursive as the contents of the field initiate or prompt another round of inquiry or thought. So I would add, as we listen we also immerse ourselves in the field of experience: a process of "becoming the field," identifying with aspects of the field.
> (Cartwright, 2013, p. 90)

My powerful reaction to Lillie felt as if I had joined an already existing experience that had yet to be fully recognized. In this context, I wish to quote Marcel Proust's insightful observation touching upon a comparable experience: "I felt myself still reliving a past which was no longer anything more than the history of another person."[1] I had imagined something instead of Lillie's mother doing so, or more precisely, as if a part of her mother's potential imagination was dissociated, could not achieve fulfillment and therefore "chose" me to be its conveyor and channel of manifestation. Indeed, a disabled woman could have big dreams for her daughter. She might wish her daughter could experience things her own disability deprived her of achieving. However, it is also possible that the daughter's ability to reach things beyond her mother's options cannot be taken for granted. These processes can be implicit and intricate; we can also speculate on the guilt Lillie might have felt because of her ability to do things that her mother couldn't. What became apparent is that Lillie surprised herself by acknowledging that she was a dancer, whereas her mother had polio. She created this connection, solidifying the disparity between those who can freely move, and those who cannot. She "knew" something deep about those two existential options and revived both of them alternately in our meetings, and my perception of her switched accordingly. Connecting the sense of creativity with maternal caregiving in early infancy, Winnicott asserts that

> Creativity, then, is the retention throughout life of something that belongs properly to infant experience: the ability to create the world. For the baby this is not difficult, because if the mother is able to adapt to the baby's needs, the baby has no initial appreciation of the fact that the world was there before he or she was conceived or conceived of. The Reality Principle is the fact of the existence of the world whether the baby creates it or not. Given good-enough environmental conditions, the individual child ... found ways of absorbing the insult. [of Reality Principle – my clarification]
>
> (1990, p. 40)

Winnicott illustrates how the quality of maternal caregiving is associated with living creatively.

> If a mother has eight children, there are eight mothers. This is not simply because of the fact that the mother was different in her attitude to each of the eight. If she could have been exactly the same with each ... each child would have had his and her own mother seen through individual eyes.
>
> (p. 40)

This sense of creating the world, as well as creating the Other, is mutual for both participants: the baby creates the mother; and the mother creates the baby. Comparing the therapeutic relationship to that of the parent–child, my double perception of Lillie may also be associated with the double internalized maternal images – one who could dream her child dancing, and the other, incapable of such imagination. It was as if I had become two different mothers, responding to two separate babies.

Sometimes I had dreams that a nondisabled mother would have dreamt of her daughter, but were not dreamt by Lillie's mother, and instead found a place in me and were imagined by me. As Bromberg puts it:

The nature of the patient/therapist relationship in analytic treatment could thus be described as a journey in which two people must each loosen the rigidity of their dissociative "truths" about self and other in order to allow "imagination" to find its shared place.

(2013, p. 1)

Discussing the functions and virtues of imagination in therapy, Bromberg quotes Winnicott (1971):

"As a patient begins to become a whole person and begins to lose her rigidly organized dissociations, she becomes aware—[because] she has a place from which to become aware—of the vital importance that fantasying has always had for her."

(p. 27, in Bromberg, 2013)

Bromberg suggests that one of Winnicott's most brilliant insights is in stating that at the same time this is happening "'the fantasying is changing into imagination . . . [and] the big differences belong to the presence or the absence of a dissociated state . . . In the fantasying, what happens, happens immediately, except that it does not happen at all'" (Winnicott, 1971, p. 27, in Bromberg).

In other words, the differences between fantasy and imagination lie in the sense of dissociation versus integrity. Bromberg notes that the self that is portrayed in fantasying is dissociated from the "me" that is having the fantasy and is essentially a different self:

It is to this different self that, just as Winnicott says, what is happening is happening immediately, except that it is not happening at all. It is not happening at all because the self that then exists—the self that is having the fantasy at that moment—cannot imagine it as "me."

(Bromberg, p. 12)

In contrast to fantasizing, a person who is imagining experiences the self as it now exists, except that it is projected into the future. Bromberg notes:

Because the self being imagined is the same self that is doing the imagining, the person as he is now has the capacity to act into a future that is real to him because the future that is imagined in the here-and-now is itself real. When the capacity to transform fantasy into imagination starts to increase, self-state transitions do not disrupt self-continuity, which in turn allows the present and the future to be bridged and thus to coexist. The person does not have to remain stuck in fantasy. What is imagined is not impossible for the self in the present; it just hasn't happened yet.

(Bromberg, p. 13)

The capacity to experience the shifts between interior and exterior realities is essential for both patients and therapists. For a prolonged period, it remained unclear to me whose imagination was, in fact, dreaming Lillie as she danced effortlessly and gracefully. Was it only my imagination that had been "taken over" or had I somehow entered into someone else's unconscious experience? Bromberg asserts that

As self-state permeability increases, so does openness to "state-sharing." The co-creation of a lived, relational unconscious increasingly nourishes the willingness of each person to participate in a growing sense of "We" that includes "Me" and "You," as part of their individually expanded self-experiences.

(p. 1)

The more my imagination attained an "objective" status, the more I let myself participate in Lillie's relational world; being invaded by her inner images enabled the shared experience necessary for the development of selfhood. According to Davies:

All of the clinician's reactions to the patient and all of the patient's reactions to the therapist are threads in the tapestry that is woven by both participants/observers to form the relational matrix within which and through which the therapy unfolds. The therapeutic relationship thus forms both the background and foreground.

(Pine, 1981, in Davies, 1994, p. 5)

Reflecting on our telephone conversation before we had ever met, I wonder if that was a form of "pregnancy" – something that had begun being imagined before it actually happened. My curiosity put me in the position of an expectant mother, waiting for her daughter to come into being. In this sense, my unwitting thought – that the woman behind the voice was "perfectly healthy" – was very much in line with the thoughts of a pregnant woman. Imagining Lillie not as someone who needed to be healed, but rather as someone whose healthiness needed to be unchained, could be the curative component in our shared journey.

Therapists' willingness to be emotionally affected by their patients' projections was highly emphasized in the neo-Kleinian, intersubjective and relational schools of thought, pointing to the therapist's ability to function as part of the patient's emotional world. The co-created experience between Lillie and me enabled an unknown desire to emerge and echo in my own imagination. This, in turn, allowed me to absorb not only what Lillie was feeling and experiencing, but also what she could potentially have been feeling and experiencing if a higher degree of motion and mobility was at hand. Such potential feeling is associated with the idea that life is worth living. Lack of physical movement was, in this case, highly associated with the futility of moving between different states, modes and in particular between internal and external realities. Thus, it was impossible for her to recognize whose paralysis she was experiencing and to understand how to extract herself from it without betraying her mother's love. This case is one of the more salient and prominent examples in which physical limitations easily become tantamount to emotional paralysis. The sense of inflexibility (both physical and emotional) well demonstrates this basic idea. The metaphoric meanings of idioms such as "to take a step," "to spread one's wings," "to act on something" and many other idioms connecting the sense of physical action with mental accomplishments, are additional examples of how primary and secondary processes are interconnected.

In Romain Gary's masterpiece *Kites* (1980), Ludo is requested to define "grace" in a single word. In response, he recalls his little Polish lover – her neck, her arms, her shining hair – and answers without hesitation: "movement."[2] This quote illustrates one central idea of psychoanalysis: that the foundation of life and mental health is related to the experience of being in motion. This moment in the novel gives us a small glimpse into Ludo's mind. One might expect that addressing the apparently scientific question "What characterizes grace?" demands a rational answer, capable of linking cause and effect. However, to explore the issue of grace, Ludo is called upon to get in touch with a different, more subjective, mode of experience – a mode in which ambiguity is not necessarily something to be deciphered, but rather an experience to be shared. The transformation he goes through after meeting his love provides him with new meanings of the word grace. When called upon to describe the magic of aesthetic, which is non-verbal, love comes to Ludo's aid. This literary example well demonstrates the mix between the artistic and the academic languages. Using *belles-lettres* helps me summarize this case, since the ability to imagine is not only the base of prose and poetry, or of mental health, but also the base of the practical therapeutic enterprise. Winnicott acknowledged it while speaking about cultural experience and its association with the transitional area, the "in-between" space. In his book *Playing and Reality*, he quoted the famous poet Rabindranath Tagore and used his poem as the introduction to the work. "On the seashore of endless worlds, children play" (Tagor, 1916). This quotation describes the borderline between worlds; the point at which the limited encounters the endless is the place of playful experiences (Winnicott, 1971, p. 112). To imagine Lillie dancing was to be in that in-between space, knowing her real history, yet imagining what was not there but only existed in the form of unrealized potential.

In the end, Lillie did not make a career out of her dancing, but she did return to dancing for her own pleasure and joy. In the spirit of my theoretical ideas presented in this book, I hope it will be correct to suggest that Lillie was "moved" by our shared journey and by my imagination. I hope this feeling was associated with her ability to move on with her life. In any case, her history may be a good example of a reverse process: a case in which one person's physical, actual limitation regarding movement might lead to a frozen state of mind in another, and vice versa. However, as I mentioned at the outset of this book, as language and primary processes are embedded in each other from the very start, at a certain point it does not matter what came first – the sense of emotional futility or the physical disability – both must be "moved." In describing the case of his male patient's penis envy, Winnicott wrote: "On this Friday he went away profoundly *moved* and feeling that this was the first significant shift in the analysis for a long time" (Winnicott, 1971, p. 73 [emphasis added]). Whereas Winnicott used the passive verb "moved" in a metaphoric manner, I suggest that in certain cases this passive verb may attain a concrete, tangible form. In a previous chapter, I related to Darwin's observations regarding the affinity between bodily behavioral gestures and idiomatic expressions. In one of his discussions Darwin linked physical passivity with the expression of emotions:

> Most of our emotions are so closely connected with their expression, that they hardly exist if the body remains passive – the nature of the expression depending in chief part on the nature of the actions which have been habitually performed under this particular state of the mind … a man may intensely hate another, but until his bodily frame is affected, he cannot be said to be enraged.
> (Darwin, 1952, pp. 237–238)

In another place, he writes that "the free expression by outward signs of an emotion intensifies it. On the other hand, the repression, as far as this is possible, of all outward signs softens our emotions" (p. 365). This idea trapped my mind while thinking about Lillie's difficulties in fulfilling her desire of dancing as associated with a frozen state of mind, as well as the possible linkage between her mother's physical limitations and its potential emotional implications. I hope my own imagination could serve as a venue in which it was possible to unchain the repressed expressions, which, in turn, allow for more degrees of freedom in both emotional and behavioral aspects.

To conclude this chapter, I quote Bromberg, who asserts that

> Imagination is above all else alive, creative, and spontaneous. In what takes place between patient and analyst, if it is allowed to thrive it facilitates a connection that enlarges the sense of wholeness in both partners without their losing any of their parts. I still see it as a miracle.
>
> (2013, p. 13)

Note

1   In Search of Lost Time. Vol. 6, *The Fugitive*.
2   Surprisingly, this novel has never been translated into English. It originally appears in French. See Gary, R. (1980) *Les cerfs-volants* (Folio), Paris: Gallimard.

References

Bromberg, P.M. (1998). *Standing in the Spaces: Essays on Clinical Process, Trauma and Dissociation*. Hillsdale, NJ: The Analytic Press.
Bromberg, P.M. (2013). Hidden in Plain Sight: Thoughts on Imagination and the Lived Unconscious, *Psychoanalytic Dialogues*, 23: 1–14.
Cartwright, D. (2013). Clinical Features of the Container Function, *Psychoanalytic Psychotherapy in South Africa*, 21(2): 73–104.
Darwin, C. (1952). *The Expression of the Emotion in Man and Animals*. Chicago, IL and London: University of Chicago Press.
Davies, J.M. (1994). *Treating the Adult Survivor of Childhood Sexual Abuse*. New York: Basic Books.
Davies, J.M. (2004). Whose Bad Objects Are We Anyway? *Psychoanalytic Dialogues*, 14: 711–732.
Gary, R. (1980). *Les cerfs-volants* (Folio), Paris: Gallimard.
Grossmark, R. (2012). The Unobtrusive Relational Analyst, *Psychoanalytic Dialogues*, 22: 629–646.
Mitchell, S.A. (1993). *Hope and Dread in Psychoanalysis*. New York: Basic Books.
Ogden, T.H. (2007). *This Art of Psychoanalysis: Dreaming Undreamt Dreams and Interrupted Cries*. New York: Routledge.

Parson, M. (2009). An Independent Theory of Clinical Technique, *Psychoanalytic Dialogues*, 19: 221–236.

Pine, F. (1981). In the Beginning: Contributions to a Psychoanalytic Developmental Psychology, *International Review of Psychoanalysis*, 8: 15–33.

Proust, M. (1927/2003). *Albertine disparue* [*The Fugitive*]. London: Penguin.

Tagore, R. (1916). *Gitanjali (Song Offerings), a Collection of Prose Translations Made by the Author from the Original Bengali*. Calcutta: Macmillan.

Winnicott, D.W. (1971). *Playing and Reality*. London: Tavistock.

Chapter 7

Travel far to draw near

One of the most surprising referrals to my clinic was that of a woman living in the northern part of the country. One day, the phone rang, and the area code of a distant settlement appeared on the screen. It caught me by surprise when, on the other end of the line, I heard a voice asking to schedule an appointment. I refrained from asking the obvious question: Why would anyone want to travel such a long distance for therapy? Instead, I was curious to meet the face behind the voice.

I will call her Ruth. Ruth sought out therapy due to a case of unrequited love. Anyone who has ever experienced unrequited love is probably familiar with the exceedingly intense feelings of longing, missing, feeling bereft, loss, despair and pain. These feelings are often accompanied by a sense of low self-esteem and the idea that life is something that exists elsewhere – far away – and is being lived by other people.

A woman in her thirties entered the room and very soon began to reveal her yearning for a man with whom she had been deeply in love with for years. "I have no life without him," Ruth told me, relating her unfathomable despair; for various reasons, she could not fulfill her love. Choking with tears, she prayed for the day when she would be able to forget him and go on with her life, which was in a state of interruption, stasis. Perhaps, Ruth felt, life did not exist for her at all. She kept listing events her unreachable, beloved man was invited to, while she stayed alone at home, lamenting her acute longing for him.

At a certain point, after discussing the emotional relationship to which she felt chained, I allowed myself to inquire about her motivation to drive such a long distance to seek mental help. At that time, it seemed as if the answer was hidden from both of us. She could not explain her choice, apart from the fact that she could not find a good enough therapist living in her area. Frankly, it was tempting for me to think that no skilled therapists of my level of expertise existed in her area. For a moment, I enjoyed the feeling of being singled out, although I still thought the whole thing was a bit strange. The thought that there was nothing of value, nothing "good enough" in the place where she lived could easily be associated with her feeling that real, meaningful life was not close at hand, but existed elsewhere, somewhere far away, where her untouchable, unattainable other resided. At that time, she believed that any attempt to live a meaningful life without him was useless. I asked her if she could see the connection between both experiences. Even though at that time, this intervention could not bridge the abyss of her pain, identifying the possible affinity between both experiences put the therapy in a desirable place – one that could "compete" with the glory of the man she loved. In other words, there was something about this identification that created a mediating space between the things that were out of her reach, and those she owned and were part of her world, such as therapy. Once a week, she traveled far to draw near, driving for three hours to come to my clinic. I started thinking about her in different ways between our sessions.

For example, while I was meeting with other patients, I knew she had started heading in my direction three hours before each of our sessions. It occurred to me that this patient's long journey toward me was beginning to extend my preoccupation with her. The distance had started attaining more and more meanings which, at this point, had yet to be fully revealed.

After her long journey, Ruth used our sessions to pave a path inside herself, down to the very depths of her soul. An intricate interplay had been established between the internal and the external, and gradually she developed a sense of familiarity regarding the limits and borders of this playground.

In one of our sessions, after talking about her broken heart for a while, she reconsidered the geographical distance. At that point, she could finally tell me definitively: she felt she could not talk about the object of her love and her feelings toward him within the geographical territory of her residential area. She had to travel far to speak about the pain of distance. She had to visually and concretely portray this distancing, and the remoteness of her experience, by consuming kilometers and gallons of gasoline and viewing the changing scenery outside of her car window. In other words: she had to travel far so she could feel near.

The Torah is crammed full of figures that have been flung far from the bosom of their community only to return and make the most impactful change. Rachel Roberts (2017) reviews the biblical figures that have undergone this process: Abraham leaves his home in Ur of the Chaldees to go forth and receive God's blessing; Jacob flees his father's house in fear of his brother and takes a journey during which he obtains spiritual insight and a new name, which becomes the patronymic of his people; Joseph, sold into slavery by his brothers, goes to Egypt and achieves greatness, ultimately returning in triumph to the family who has rejected him; Elijah flees to the mountains after crossing the pagan queen, Jezebel, and then hears a still, small voice that rescues his people from their wicked leaders; and Moses lives in the palace of Pharaoh, the oppressor of the Israelites, before leading them to freedom. However, this is not the case regarding Ruth. In addition to the many differences, all of the above examples portray historical leaders – male protagonists, who take charge not only of their own lives but of the entire community. It is beyond the scope of this chapter to review the way history (and the Bible as well) deals differently with male and female protagonists, and this has already been discussed in other works. However, when dealing with the relations between the sexes, it is impossible to ignore the more comprehensive social context, even today, in the 21st century. Ruth's fundamental, basic experience – undervaluing her own life – may be seen as carrying both personal and social meanings. My attempt here is to relate to both, as they are highly interwoven with one another.

A large body of material in psychoanalytic literature has been dedicated to the different kinds of love and the possible connections between unfulfilled love and mourning. This has been done since the age of Freud, through the various branches of object relations theories. The status of the feminine voice is also a topic that continues to preoccupy psychoanalysis in multiple, diverse ways, too numerous to be summed up here. In the context of dealing with the relations between concrete and metaphoric aspects of human experience, I choose to quote Kristeva, who focuses on love and the feminine voice, a relevant subject in this case.

Kristeva focuses her approach on what she calls the "semiotic," the pre-lingual communication between mother and child, which is prior to the Oedipal phase (Kristeva, 1987a). In contrast to Lacan, who views the individual's initiation into symbolic language as a separation from the mother, Kristeva suggests that pre-linguistic experiences regarded as "maternal" are not lost after the individual enters the social order, but are restored and revived in different contexts. Whereas the values governing symbolic language are those of order, clarity, hierarchy and stability, the *semiotic* is a mode of communication that undermines this order, subverts authority, refuses hierarchy and rejects clarity. Kristeva asserts that any creation of meaning is a mix of the symbolic and the semiotic. Without the semiotic, the symbolic order would have no real meaning.

Looking at the case presented here through this lens, we can perceive the unique, semiotic mode of expression Ruth used to describe her unrequited love – a mode of expression that glorified the male figure while depriving herself of a sense of selfhood and subjectivity. It was as if everything longed for, desired, worshiped and adored was his, while she was left wounded, absent, empty-handed and bereft. Of course, there are also many cases in which men fall apart over women. However, these cases deserve a separate discussion, as we cannot ignore the social reality that favors masculinity over femininity. Hence, her unfulfilled love was not merely a matter of an unattained man, but rather a painful encounter with her feelings of inferiority, her sense of being erased and delegitimized.

Ruth's weekly journey to my clinic was her semiotic way to voice her pain, uttered in various articulated and intricate non-verbal manners. She had chosen to measure the distance between her love and her faraway beloved man in kilometers, as well as the gap between what existed within her own territory and that which was distant and alien. However, the truly significant issue was her choice to express the enormous distance gaping in her soul through other parameters, apart from words. The wheels' motion on the highway, the changing scenery reflected outside her car window, the songs on the radio, the chains of thoughts and associations which accompanied her on her journey and the many other physical features that marked her way – were all parts of the map, the route of her experience.

In her book *Strangers to Ourselves* (1991), Kristeva uses the second person narrative mode to discuss the "foreigner." She connects silence with femininity:

> ... it is not the silence of anger that jostles words at the edge of the idea and the mouth; rather, it is the silence that empties the mind and fills the brain with despondency, like the gaze of sorrowful women coiled up in some nonexistent eternity.
>
> (p. 16)

However, as she asserts in other works, there are other modes of expression that undermine symbolic speech and are maternal. Among the various ways to trace these modes, I find poetry to be the most fitting arena for the conjunction between the two modes of expressions – the linguistic and the semiotic – as it uses words to touch (double meaning) upon primary experiences, and is therefore of therapeutic value. As Anna Smith reminds us, "Philosophy and literature have sought procedures that would estrange the object of perception in order to render it paradoxically more beautiful, more knowable, or both" (1996, p. 3).

For me, poetry and prose are not merely subjects of inquiry. As objects of aesthetic inspiration, they expand the boundaries of my daily life – personal as well as professional – allowing me a more creative, ongoing process of coping with my life and my patients. As Zoran reminds us, the idea that literature has a healing potential is as old as literature itself. Inscribed over the door of the ancient libraries at Thebes and Alexandria were the words: "Healing Place of the Soul" (ΨΥΧΗΣ ΙΑΤΡΕΙΟΝ). We also know of the famous debate between Plato and Aristotle about literature, in which Plato practically expels the poets from his ideal state, while Aristotle implicitly defends them by developing the concept of "catharsis," which refers to the healing influence of tragedy on its audience (Zoran, 2000). Here, I choose to quote the first phrase of a poem penned by Ra'hel, the poetess. I realized that it inspired me in my capacity to be in an ambiguous state, from which I could better connect with Ruth. The name of the poem is *Melancholic Song*[1]:

> Will you hear my voice, my faraway one?
> Will you hear it from afar, wherever you are?

The feminine narrator of this poem turns to her far-off, beloved man (in Hebrew the gender of the addressee is masculine) in a very personal, intimate and direct tone. Despite the apparently simple utterance, an articulated, shrewd and hidden idea is implied in these seemingly plain lines. The question "Will you hear my voice, my faraway one?" creates the oxymoronic, apparently surprising, combination "my faraway." Although "far" and "mine" do not naturally go together, the moment they are unified, consolidated in the poem's domain, the avowed becomes the removed, far-off one, and the distant becomes the object of desire. However, the surprising and unexpected experience encapsulated in this combination is not merely a matter of semantics (identifying the distant with the owned). It is rather the feminine mode of expression rebelling against structural axioms and undermining clear order, violating the act of making sense and reminding us that beyond the well-known linguistic rules, other – perhaps feminine – possibilities are at hand. Possibilities that cross and violate geographical and linguistic borders, and are capable of creating new and surprising neologisms. In Hebrew, the words *my faraway one* are encapsulated by Ra'hel in one word (*rehoki*), thereby creating an innovative linguistic neologism. This neologism is not apparent at first glance, as the harmonic rhyming, phonic texture, and sounds mask the complexities and violent clashes between two opposing forces – the symbolic linguistic order, and the semiotic. The feminine narrator feels absent and bereft. She has to find her own way to express her longing for her masculine, faraway beloved, a way that could also be understood by him; meaning, through the fine, symbolic order of language. Therefore, the phrase "wherever you are" may be regarded not only as a matter of physical location, but also as a linguistic matter or, more precisely, an existential matter that may be revealed through an entirely different mode of expression. Mixing these two modes of expression in this poem of love and longing serves as a bridge between the sexes, creating a new existential option. In such a world, "far" can become "mine." As Anna Smith puts it: "Poetic language could then be seen as an entity that challenged linguistic paradigms without acceding to them" (1996, p. 4). Addressing Kristeva's concept of estrangement, Smith asserts that for Kristeva, poetic language was the key to estranging perception and, more ambitiously, all thought, because it introduced a heterogeneous space into signifying structures and subjective identity. Poetic language transmuted the ecstasy of the visionary or mystic experience outside language into an ecstatic experience within language: "'a fire of tongues,' an exit from representation" (Kristeva, 1987b, p. 253). Smith further notes:

> ... language already contains the potential for its own Pentecostal renewal: what she terms "the fire of tongues." When language became dense with phonic textures and semantic associations, that is, when it became poetic, it acted as an entry-point for the drives to transfer their psychic imprints from the unconscious directly into significations, causing it to falter and renew itself.
>
> (p. 5)

Kristeva addresses the foreigner: "Your speech, fascinating as it might be on account of its very strangeness, will be of no consequence, will have no effect, will cause no improvement in the image or reputation of those you are conversing with" (1991, p. 20). Indeed, this is exactly what the feminine narrator in Ra'hel's poem is asking: *Will you hear my voice?* However, her answer is developed in the question itself, as the question is formulated in a somehow semiotic manner, being asked in a paradoxical oxymoronic fashion, subverting the fine linguistic order, crying out for recognition without speaking the language of the citizen who owns the territory of symbolic words. The woman in Rachel's poem implores the masculine addressee in a very personal tone: 'Will you hear my voice?' Here, I draw upon Kristeva's concept of exile. She poses the question: "How can one avoid sinking into the mire of common sense, if not by becoming a stranger to one's own country, language, sex and identity writing is impossible without some kind of exile?" (Kristeva, 1987b). Smith mentions that

> for Kristeva, the call of writing demands that the exile refuses to take comfort in narcissistic regression to maternal origins or in clinging to a singular identity. Subjectivity is heterogeneous, and the exile is most at home with an intolerable excess in language that leads away from the representation of one's sexual identity, for instance, to affect multiple sublations of the unnamable, the unrepresented, the void.
>
> (Smith, 1996, p. 5)

Ra'hel's poem acknowledges the gap between two kinds of realms, which may also be termed masculine and feminine. However, these polarities go far beyond the differences between the sexes. The poem is not aimed at minimizing this distance. Rather, it attempts to acknowledge it in both content and form. On the content level, it speaks about this distance. On the form level, the poetic level, it uses idiosyncratic language, so that the feminine narrator can address her faraway one while retaining her own identity, without losing herself in his territory, and still communicatively express her longing and desire. This is exactly what Ruth needed. As Smith says of Kristeva:

> There are periods in her writing when femininity is linked to the destabilizing qualities of poetic language (the semiotic) . . . while the quest for estrangement in one sense dissolves sexual identities, at other times, she has granted women exemplary status as strangers and exiles, whose place on the margins of public discourse potentially gives them a special indifference to the mire of common sense.
>
> (p. 6)

The dialectic in Ra'hel's poem takes place not merely between far and near, man and woman. It is also a discourse between languages, between different modes of expression or, in Kristeva's terminology, between the semiotic and the symbolic. The feminine mode of expression voices itself in its own unique fashion.

Kristeva suggests that

> the ear is receptive to conflicts only when the body loses its footing. A certain imbalance is necessary, a swaying over some abyss, for a

conflict to be heard. Yet when the foreigner – the speech-denying strategist – does not utter his conflict, he in turn takes root in his own world of a rejected person whom no one is supposed to hear.

(1991, p. 17)

Ruth felt that only in a far-off place could she share her closest and most intimate feelings. Exile was her default mode, her most familiar place. Therefore, driving so far away each time made the experience of exile more present, a closer and more genuine reflection of her inner experience.

She used the long hours of driving to think about herself and her life, to increase the distance from one destination, on her way to another. The goal was not to bridge the gap which, as said, was unbridgeable, but to figuratively mark it, to make it present and concrete, to inscribe her desire on the highway. The therapeutic discourse did not call for love redemption. Rather, it aimed to re-establish Ruth's presence, unfold her subjectivity as a mode of expression, experience and existence. In addition, it was an attempt to regain ownership of her feelings of love and sense of selfhood, to validate her love as an internal celebration, nurtured by something more than a disappointing, inaccessible external object. However, alongside her pre-verbal mode of expression, she used our sessions to *speak*. In so doing (driving far to speak near) she created an original and new combination of both modes of expression. An intermediate area, a liminal space of peripheral experiences, had been unfolded.

Gradually, Ruth was able to talk more and more about herself. Her longings for her distant lover could now be conceptualized in terms of earlier wounds. Childhood memories, longings and wishes for recognition became increasingly more available to her; characters, events and various experiences began to take shape in our sessions. Acknowledging the emerging themes associated with her love, including longing and desire, as part of her own world – not his – slowly became possible.

Benjamin refers to the concept of domination to understand the relations between the sexes. In contrast to Freud, who imagined the origins of civilization in the primal struggle between father and son, Benjamin views domination as the subordination of women by men internalized by both sexes:

> The struggle for power takes place between father and son; woman plays no part in it, except as prize or temptation to regression, or as the third point of a triangle . . . Indeed, woman's subordination to man is taken for granted, invisible.
>
> (Benjamin, 1988, pp. 6–7)

She further asserts that

> the point of departure for this reexamination of the problem of domination is Simone de Beauvoir's insight: that woman functions as man's primary other, his opposite – playing nature to his reason, immanence to his transcendence, primordial oneness to his individuated separateness, and object to his subject.
>
> (p. 7)

Social context and its implications on the psychological developments of both men and women go far beyond the current discussion. However, it is not the first time in my private practice, as well as in so many other arenas, that painful experiences of unrequited love are deeply associated with a sense of a lack of recognition, and this holds true in a much broader social and relational context. As Benjamin asserts, "recognition is so central to human existence as to often escape notice; or, rather, it appears to us in so many guises that it is seldom grasped as one overarching concept" (p. 15). This

> longing for recognition lies beneath the sensationalism of power and powerlessness, so that the unrecognizable forms often taken by our desire are the result of a complicated but ultimately understandable process – a process which explains how our deepest desires for freedom and communion become implicated in control and submission.
>
> (p. 84)

In fact, I could present this case in so many different ways. Every analytic endeavor is, in a way, a journey into the unknown, endless possible paths stretching in infinite directions, and requires us to make our choices about which path to take. Here, I seek to decipher the subversive meanings hidden behind Ruth's unique mode of expression in her choice to travel such a distance to reach my clinic, and view them as an act of unfolding feminine selfhood. I strive to focus on the poetic meanings of her choice and view them as an impactful mode of expression, which portrays Ruth as an individual capable of subjectively voicing her desires, from her own point of view, and using her own kind of language.

Benjamin argues that

> too often, woman's desire is expressed through such alienated forms of submission and envy, the products of idealization. This process of

alienation works, in part, through the transformation of recognition from the concrete intersubjective mode to the symbolic phallic mode, in which recognition is not subject-to-object but occurs through identification with the ideal; and the erotic relationship is organized into the complementarity of active and passive organs, subject and object of desire.

(p. 131)

Ruth was both imprisoned in, and barred from, the world of her far-off love object. The first step was the ability to rebel against the axiomatic assumptions she held regarding her sense of inferiority. Our aim was not for her to stop missing her beloved, but rather, to unchain her feminine experience, which, as I saw it, couldn't be separated from the broader social context. As Benjamin asserts, ". . . it is precisely because women have been deprived of early identificatory love, the erotic force behind separation, that they are so often unable to forge the crucial link between desire and freedom" (p. 132).

Despite any differences existing between the approaches of Benjamin and Kristeva, both challenge masculine psychoanalytic models regarding the relations between the sexes and women being subordinated to a masculine perspective – a topic that has attained more and more attention in recent decades. One major challenge in our psychotherapeutic endeavor was to accompany Ruth on her quest to attain her own identity and her own desires.

Benjamin relates to the fact that the route to individuality, via identificatory love of the father, is a difficult one for women to follow. The difficulty lies in the fact that the power of the liberator-father is used as a defense against the engulfing mother. Thus, however helpful a specific change in the father's relationship with the daughter may be in the short run, it cannot solve the deeper problem: the split between a father of liberation and a mother of dependency. Understanding desire, as the desire for recognition, changes our view of the erotic experience. It enables us to describe a mode of representing desire unique to intersubjectivity which, in turn, offers a new perspective on woman's desire (Benjamin, 1988, p. 126).

Obviously, Ruth was pleading for recognition. She was trapped in the idea that there was only one place that could reaffirm her existence, and this was a masculine, inaccessible place. However, additional options gradually rose to the surface.

One may wonder: Can therapy conducted by a female therapist be capable of providing this recognition and reassurance?

Benjamin asserts that the daughter's love for her father leads to erotic submission, as she needs him to recognize her subjectivity, initiation, independence, otherness and femininity. She wants him to provide her with herself. Identificatory love is one step in developing her feminine self, as a way of identifying what is needed for the wholeness of this self, and in the hope that recognition occurs through love and surrender. If the father's love is accomplished, it is the first stage of the daughter's recognition of herself, as a subject similar to the father. However, if the father ignores her need, she remains "stuck" in the model of erotic submission, in a master–slave relationship, continuously emptying out for the idealized man. She is trapped in a masochistic mode.

Could these premises be associated with the question "Will you hear my voice, my faraway one?" raised in Ra'hel's poem? This question reflects a personal, feminine voice. The poem does not provide an answer. It avoids deciding whether this desire could, in fact, be met or not. And answering the question is not really what is important. Rather, it is the posing of the question in itself, which is of importance, meaning: the capacity to bear the loss, to tolerate that which is missing, to echo this absence without striving to fulfill it. This kind of phraseology may echo the more authentic sense of absence, therefore enabling a sense of subjectivity – not by means of being fulfilled, but by creating a new space, featured by longing and desire.

So different from one another, Kristeva and Benjamin, as well as many other feminist thinkers, challenged the priority of the symbolic order and brought into the psychoanalytic literature concepts and ideas related to feminine subjectivity and gender relations. What I find impactful in the case presented in this chapter is the mode of expression through which Ruth "chose" to express her desire. Can we call it semiotic? She had to travel far to reach a place where she could talk about her love. Does this distance perhaps mark her escape from a territory in which she was trapped in a man's world – the world of her unattainable lover?

Benjamin undermines the polarized perception that identifies the father as the route towards rationality and individuation, whereas the mother is identified as threatening the individual's subjectivity and freedom. Instead, she views this split as emerging from our gender relations. This sociopsychological fact demands deconstruction. In this context, Ruth's choice to drive not only far away, but also towards a female therapist, is interesting. It seems as though her turning from masculinity to femininity was not simply consciously made. Rather, her mode of expression, which can be regarded as semiotic, and in which the somatic, non-verbal prevails – with its wheels driving on the road, bridging the abyss dividing foreign territories – was impactful. As in poetry, by prising off the carapace of routine, her idiosyncratic style allowed for the emergence of a new experience.

At the end of one of our sessions, with one foot out the door, she glanced back at me and smiled: "Undoubtedly," she remarked, "if ever asked about my therapy, I will say that I have come a long way . . ."

Note

1   Ra'hel the poetess is the pen name of Rachel Bluwstein Sela, a Hebrew-language poet who immigrated to Palestine (then part of the Ottoman Empire) in 1909. Most of her poems were written in the final six years of her life, while suffering from tuberculosis. Ra'hel is known for her lyrical style, the brevity of her poems, and the revolutionary simplicity of her conversational tone. Many of her poems echo her feelings of longing and loss, a result of her inability to realize her aspirations in life. She was the first Jewish woman poet in Israel to receive recognition in a genre that was practiced solely by men. Anthologies of her poetry remain bestsellers to this day, and her influence on modern day Israelis is unquestionable. The woman described in this case was familiar with Ra'hel's poetry, as it is a well-known part of Israeli culture and education. Most of Ra'hel's poems have never been translated into English, except for of one collection of selected poems, translated to English by Robert Friend. The phrase quoted in this chapter is the first stanza of a longer poem, which has never been translated into English. I translated it myself, specifically for this book.

References

Benjamin, J. (1988). *The Bonds of Love: Psychoanalysis, Feminism, and the Problem of Domination.* New York: Pantheon.
Kristeva, J. (1987b). *In the Beginning was Love: Psychoanalysis and Faith.* A. Goldhammer (Trans.). New York: Columbia University Press.
Kristeva, J. (1987b). *Tales of Love.* New York: Columbia University Press.
Kristeva, J. (1991). *Strangers to Ourselves.* L.S. Roudiez (Trans.). New York: Columbia University Press.
Ra'hel the Poetess. (1995). *Flowers of Perhaps, Selected Poems of Ra'hel.* R. Friend (Trans.). London: Menard Publisher.
Roberts, R. (2017). Acherei Mot-Kedoshim: Travel Far to Draw Near. Available at: https://medium.com/ifnotnowtorah/acherei-mot-kedoshim-travel-far-to-draw-near-f1fa808f227. Retrieved on 17/7/2017.
Smith, A. (1996). *Julia Kristeva – Readings of Exile and Estrangement.* New York: St. Martin's.
Zoran, R. (2000). *The Third Voice: The Therapeutic Qualities of Literature and their Application in Bibliotherapy.* Jerusalem: Carmel [Hebrew].

Chapter 8

On the record
The possibility of publicly disclosing cases of sexual abuse

Writing this chapter was extremely difficult for me. The endeavor of combining words into sentences and sentences into ideas was emotionally taxing work. I found myself suffering while attempting to carry out the task of disclosing the topic with which this chapter deals; lines and phrases were written and deleted many times. And, most interestingly, alongside the process of writing, another motive frequently appeared: the desire to put my ideas down on paper – quickly – and then shelve them, and never let this chapter see the light of day. Only in retrospect could I identify this attitude as deviating from the regular, familiar difficulty that usually accompanies the process of publishing articles. Only in retrospect I realized that this was the point and that this kind of suffering – the intense inner dilemma regarding the possibility and legitimacy of exposing certain things – was an integral part of the topic presented here: the worlds of patients struggling with an early, secret trauma. This secrecy is experienced not only as something that must not be told but rather as something that cannot be told – an unspeakable arena, residing outside the territory of words.

I am talking about patients who are survivors of early childhood sexual abuse. The experiences related to this complicated reality continue to influence them throughout their lives, accompanied by far-reaching implications. The agony I experienced in writing this chapter reflects my patient's difficulty to know and own something about her inner world, due to the mechanisms of dissociation and denial, frequently characterizing sexually abused survivors or, to put it in Bromberg's words: "it helped me know her inside out" (Bromberg, 1991). I have decided to use my personal tribulations in an attempt to harness their creative potential and to further explore the therapist's difficulty to not only intellectually understand the experiences of trauma survivors, but also to deeply and emotionally "know" something about them. In this context, my writing torments were a necessary evil –

not only for finding the appropriate way in which to write about this sensitive issue but also as a way of experiencing the quality involved in the danger of breaching borders. In this sense, I concur with Bromberg, who asserts that ". . . the analyst's change is, to one degree or another, an actual therapeutic process . . ." (Bromberg, 2013, p. 8).

The process of writing in itself, including the various emotions involved, helped me to reach a deeply internal insight, in a way that was not previously accessible to me.

My patient, whom I will call Miriam, was raised solely by her father. Her mother passed away when she was a baby, and her father routinely sexually abused her since the age of six. This memory was not recovered during therapy. It was an experience that was always in her consciousness and was further validated by other relatives as well as by the father himself, who confessed later in his life. Whenever Miriam described these memories, she fell into despair and refused to be comforted. She repeatedly said: "Certain kinds of pain are not repairable. These pains go with you to your grave." I used to think about this difficult sentence, relating to the early experiences that had left a mark on her entire life, as an invitation to rethink the clinical psychotherapeutic enterprise: its goals, features, limitations and the requisite discretion the profession demands.

Miriam was extremely lonely. She never married, had no children and no intimate friendships or familial relations. She could not associate pleasure or enjoyment with having relationships with men. She held a permanent job which enabled her to make a good living; most days, though, she barricaded herself in her home without the benefit of any contact with real friends. There were several people with whom she had different forms of interactions, some of them affectionate, but ordinarily, she preferred her own company. She usually experienced other people as too talkative, babblers and prattlers, gossiping, minding other people's business and forever failing to understand her.

Psychotherapy is especially challenging in such situations and involves various aspects and complexities. A major complexity is the overlapping issues of secrets, disclosures and protection in therapeutic relations, and the question of benefits versus dangers in writing about this kind of therapy and its disclosure to readers or any external audience. Contemplating the disclosure of such of secrets leads us to quote Davies, who writes about the sexual abuse of children, which is shrouded in secrecy and denial:

> Secrecy is imposed by the perpetrator with a variety of intimidations that range from the subtle to the viciously sadistic. Frequently, the

silence obtained from the child is so deeply internalized that the victim reaches adulthood with the secret of her violations intact. At more extreme levels of preservation, the sexual abuse remains dissociated from the everyday consciousness of the patient, thus constituting a secret even from the victim herself. If, on the other hand, the child does disclose the abuse while it is occurring, she is often ignored, disbelieved, vilified, or further abused rather than validated and supported ... If secrecy is the mainstay of childhood sexual abuse, disclosure to a validating, believing other is the first step in a process of healing the devastating wounds of early sexual victimization. It is therefore crucial that clinicians know how and when to facilitate disclosure, so that they can become that, often first, validating and believing other.

(1994, p. 86)

However, whereas speaking about the unspeakable is sometimes of curative potential, doing it inappropriately might reproduce the experience of intrusively violating the self's limits. The parallel between the inner drama of sexually abused patients regarding the status of secrets, and the therapist's dilemma regarding writing about these cases, will be shortly discussed in the context of the unique nature of transference and countertransference, which often occurs with patients struggling with early traumas.

An important vehicle by which to understand the process of what occurs within the framework of the therapeutic relations is the inner attitude of the therapist. Her thoughts, emotions and even behaviors and acts are evoked in response to the patients' projected material or, more accurately, as part of the co-created experience with her patients. Miriam invested a great deal of effort in shielding herself from inappropriate infiltration, protecting herself from the experience of dangerous, intrusive and painful contact; using the therapist's subjective feelings might provide valuable information regarding the patient's inner world. This information is essential when the verbal realm is not available for the description of profound and primary experiences. In so doing, I apply a relational model, which implies the co-creation of a shared transitional space in which both therapist and patient are free to reenact, create context and meaning, and ultimately recreate, in newly configured forms, the central, organizing relational matrices of the patient's early life. Applying a relational model to working with sexual abuse survivors, Davies has pointed out that here, the unique history, system of identifications, and fantasies specific to each participant in the therapeutic dialogue define that person's experience of the treatment and, at the same time, infuse the other participant's understanding and organization of meaning. Within the treatment model, we hold no illusion regarding the therapist's 'neutrality' and fully expect the clinician to be pulled, through transferential pressures from the patient and her own countertransferial reactions to the clinical material, into constant and ever-shifting reenactment. These are analyzed within the treatment. Such reenactments involve the unconscious recreation in the treatment setting of dissociatively unavailable aspects of self and object representation – aspects that cannot be verbally described but can, via projective-introjective mechanisms, particularly projective-identification, volley back and forth between patient and therapist in startling reconstructions of early trauma, their fantasied elaborations, and their ultimate infiltration into present-day interpersonal relationships. Within this model, reenactments are crucial, and the working-through process only clears the way for other reenactments, and still others after that. Therapeutic neutrality, in this model, lies in the clinicians' capacity to keep such reenactments fluid and ever changing, in their ability to prevent countertransference reactions from embedding the treatment in the perseverative reenactment of only one internalized self and object relationship at the expense of all others.

(p. 3)

I shall now illustrate how the above ideas were manifested in the case study presented here.

An interesting issue was raised during our therapy when Miriam asked me to present her case to the general public. At that time, I had a weekly radio broadcast in which I talked about various professional aspects of psychotherapy, and she asked me to talk about her in one of my programs. Needless to say, this request was deeply meaningful as it deviated from the usual confidential psychotherapy setting, inviting me to share information with the outside world, the public domain. On the overt level, one could understand the educational and social reasoning behind the desire to expose the extremely harmful particulars of sexual assault and sexually abusive behavior. From this perspective, talking about my patient on the radio might indeed serve to raise social awareness and perhaps help prevent the recurrence of this phenomenon. In other words, this preventive action might save other potential victims from "certain kinds of pain, which are not repairable." However, assuming that everything that takes place within the patient–therapist relationship carries hidden meanings, I felt as if I were being invited to carefully listen to her request, to journey more deeply into her secret realm and the secret, indeed, played a central role.

In her book *Trauma and Recovery* (1992), Judy Lewis Herman asserts that regarding the issue of sexual abuse, secrecy and denial characterize not only the victims, but society at large, as well as the difficulty of acknowledging this reality. She asserts that

> the ordinary response to atrocities is to banish them from consciousness. Certain violations of the social compact are too terrible to utter aloud: this is the meaning of the word unspeakable. Atrocities, however, refuse to be buried. Equally as compelling as the desire to deny atrocities is the conviction that denial does not work. Folk wisdom is filled with ghosts who refuse to rest in their graves until their stories are told – murder will out. Remembering and telling the truth about terrible events are prerequisites for the restoration of the social order and the healing of individual victims. The conflict between the will to deny horrible events and the will to proclaim them aloud is the central dialectic of psychological trauma. People who have survived atrocities often tell their stories in a highly emotional, contradictory, and fragmented manner which undermines their credibility and thereby serves the twin imperatives of truth-telling and secrecy. When the truth is finally recognized, survivors can begin their recovery. But far too often secrecy prevails, and the story of the traumatic event surfaces not as a verbal narrative but as a symptom ... denial, repression, and dissociation operate on a social as well as an individual level.
>
> (pp. 1–2)

I told myself that talking about such secrets on the radio might serve to break the silence as a form of talking "on the record," rather than off the record. Putting this topic high on the general public's agenda, as a matter of significant social relevancy, could be considered a corrective action and serve to raise social awareness. Lewis-Herman notes that the study of psychological trauma has an "underground" history:

> Like traumatized people, we have been cut off from the knowledge of our past. Like traumatized people, we need to understand the past in order to reclaim the present and the future. Therefore, an understanding of psychological trauma begins with rediscovering history. Clinicians

know the privileged moment of insight when repressed ideas, feelings, and memories surface into consciousness.

(p. 2)

Davies also notes that

throughout its history, psychoanalysis has struggled to decide what importance should be given to the role of actual childhood psychopathology. Like the larger society, psychoanalysis discovered, denied, rediscovered, redenied, and is currently discovering yet again the significance of childhood sexual trauma as an etiological factor in later psychopathology. However, even when analytic thinkers have agreed that actual early trauma is an important pathogenic phenomenon, they have disagreed on how traumatic event are internalized by the child and expressed by the adult patient. Thus, treatment models vary widely.

(1994, p. 11)

Herman quotes Freud, who concluded that "at the bottom of every case of hysteria there are *one or more occurrences of premature sexual experience*" (Freud, 1896, p. 203, in Herman, p. 13). However later, and despite Freud's acknowledgment of the reality of his patients' experiences, in the famous case of Dora he refused to validate Dora's feelings of outrage and humiliation. Instead, he insisted upon exploring her feelings of erotic excitement, as if the exploitative situation were a fulfillment of her desire. When Dora broke off the treatment, Freud interpreted it as revenge (p. 14). Herman shows how the dominant psychological theory of the next century was founded upon the denial of women's reality. Sexuality remained the central focus of inquiry, but the exploitative social context in which sexual relations actually occur became utterly invisible. Psychoanalysis became a study of the internal vicissitudes of fantasy and desire, dissociated from the reality of experience. By the first decade of the twentieth century, without ever offering any clinical documentation of false complaints, Freud had concluded that his hysterical patients' accounts of childhood sexual abuse were untrue (p. 14). Was this withdrawal from his earlier formulations based solely on the social-political context of his time, or did it express trauma-related processes, which besides the wish to expose the truth also endeavored to keep the secret?

It is possible that by asking me to present her story in public, Miriam was entrusting me with her dilemma, complete with all the agony and anxiety involved in the act of disclosing the secret. Through the mechanism of projective identification, this was her way to not only tell me about her secret but also to let me "know" something further about it – to let me feel it and be a more active, intimate part of it.

Adopting a relational view in treating adult survivors of childhood sexual abuse, Davies subscribes to the thinking of Winnicott (1947), Khan (1960; 1969), Gill (1982), Mitchell (1988), Greenberg (1991), Hoffman (1991) and Bromberg (1991), among others, "all of whom stress that the clinician not only observes but also participates in the patient's relational world, actively reenacting with the patient early relational paradigms" (Davies, 1994, p. 4). The process I went through during my writing was not merely an intellectual one. There were days when I felt guilty for using my patient's history to advance my own career. At that point I had decided not to publish it, as I suspected my own motives; I blamed myself for lack of ethics. Not only, I thought, did my patient suffer from an abusive father, now she would be the victim of an abusive therapist. I felt strongly that we were both trapped at an impasse. If I were to decide to broadcast her most sensitive secrets via mass media, it would be an abusive act on my part, a vulgar and intrusive penetration into her most private realm. However, not revealing the secret would be a continuation of what she had experienced throughout her entire life: bowing to the world of secrecy and closed doors.

It took me some time to realize that my sudden feelings of guilt and shame were part of Miriam's relational world. Moreover, being controlled by these feelings, letting them dissuade me from publishing the case, was also something my patient "knew" at a very deep level. Of course, it was possible to confirm, validate and acknowledge her story within the secure zone of psychotherapy, without sharing it with the media. In many ways, this choice would be much more reasonable. Yet, this was not what she was asking from me. It was as if she brought upon us the experience that protecting her is not an obvious task, and that dangers are lurking not only outside, but rather among ourselves, inside the "family." It also would have been possible for me to show respect and understanding for her request, and strive to decipher its meanings without actually acting on it. However, it seemed as if she needed something more intrusive, more powerful, something that would blast apart the placidity of routine acceptance she had known her entire life – a deep need to shake the foundations of her story and change the scene entirely. This time, delving back into the past abuse would have a purpose, a deeper meaning; through exposure, change would come. In an attempt to broaden the conception of witnessing in analytic work with traumatized patients, Reis (2009) suggests expanding the idea to incorporate the patient's developing and varied capacity for witnessing, as well as a witnessing that occurs within the analytic relationship itself. He comes up with the idea that

> Actions occurring as part of traumatic repetition are understood to represent memory phenomena and are distinguished from dissociated self-state experience. These experiences are not therapeutically intended to be symbolized, but rather lived-through with the analyst, thus transforming the patient's own relation to the experience. . . . the scene in which this living-through takes place is the transference–countertransference matrix, and that it is the analytic encounter that allows traumatic repetition to take on the quality of a communication, an address to another, rather than remain meaningless reproduction.
> (Reiss, 2009, p. 1359)

With this in mind, it seems that her request "invited" me to act on something and thus take an active part in a certain form of communication in which "actions occur as part of traumatic repetition," using Reis' terminology.

I had to allow myself to be in contact with these "conflicted" parts of myself long enough to allow an early experience to emerge.

Davies adopts Fairbairn's view (1943) that

> the intensity of attachments to 'bad' abusive objects is particularly tenacious. Adult survivors of childhood sexual abuse, with their intense ties to abusive others, actively and with great determination and despair draw the therapist into reenactment of their chaotic early relationships. Successful treatment, therefore, depends on the therapist's ability to freely engage in these transference-countertransference reenactments and then disengage sufficiently to observe, contain, and process with the patient what has occurred between them . . . our therapeutic model is based, therefore, on a constant volleying between regressive reenactment and interpretation of that which is revived through the transference and countertransference constellations that emerge and the progressive unfolding of a new object relationship that takes place between patient and therapist during the course of treatment. Reenactment, counterbalanced by interpretation, resulting in a progressively new kind of interpersonal experience becomes the ultimate goal.
> (Davies, 1994, p. 4)

Struggling with the dilemma of whether or not to talk about Miriam's story on the radio (as well as whether or not to write this chapter), I needed enough time to allow myself to endure my related feelings of guilt and shame. Only after doing so could I reconsider the ethical issues, allowing my dilemma to attain a more rational quality. It was as if I were alternately moving from an internal to an external reality, carefully weighing the prices of each option. On the "pros" list, I thought about the importance of telling the story, especially after my patient had clearly asked me to do so, thereby clarifying her needs and desires. Davies relates to similar situations in therapy and the unique characteristics of treating sexual abuse survivors:

> When, as a child, a patient disclosed her secret to an adult who then failed to intervene or protect her, she, of course, was abused once again. Furthermore, the fantasy that someone would protect her if only she told was dismantled, leaving her even more alienated and bereft. ... clearly, the child who disclosed her sexual abuse when she was young and met with a negative response often becomes an adult patient, who, even if she remembers the sexual traumas, is terrified of disclosing again only to be rejected once more, it is the therapist's sensitivity to and comfort with derivatives and symptoms suggestive of a history of sexual trauma that can lead to disclosure and the beginning of healing.
>
> (p. 87)

Herman describes the secrecy and undergrounding encompassing the late nineteenth century studies of sexual trauma.

> At the time of these investigations there was no awareness that violence is a routine part of women's sexual and domestic lives. Freud glimpsed this truth and retreated in horror. ... not until the women's liberation movement of the 1970s was it recognized that the most common post-traumatic disorders are those not of men in war, but of women in civilian life. The real conditions of women's lives were hidden in the sphere of the personal, in private life. The cherished value of privacy created a powerful barrier to consciousness and rendered women's reality practically invisible. To speak about experiences in sexual or domestic life was to invite public humiliation, ridicule, and disbelief. Women were silenced by fear and shame, and the silence of women gave license to every form of sexual and domestic exploitation. Women did not have a name for the tyranny of private life. It was difficult to

recognize that a well-established democracy in the public sphere could coexist with conditions of primitive autocracy or advanced dictatorship in the home.

(1992, p. 28)

This approach enabled me to better understand Miriam's request to disclose her story in public, within the context of the importance of revealing the truth and finally putting an end to the ongoing concealment – on both the social and the individual level. I slowly came to understand that discussing her past experiences in our own dyadic therapy was not enough. She needed something bigger. She needed her voice to be heard by others, out loud, not behind closed doors, not off the record, but rather – for once – "on the record." Making the statement would finally make a difference. Davies further reminds us that

one of the most important therapeutic processes that occurs during treatment with survivors of childhood sexual abuse is the remembering, speaking aloud and integration of often long warded-off traumatic memories. This is conceptualized best as speaking the unspeakable and naming the unnamable.

(1994, p. 96)

Talking about Miriam's story on the radio forced me to do more than simply listen to her story. It forced me to organize the material, communicate it to others, think deeply about every single detail, consider what to say and what to refrain from saying and how, precisely, to convey this information. It was a commitment: I set out on a journey into both her history and her future at the same time. Finally, I was forced to "visit" her locked, isolated fortress, dispatch the messages from it to the external surroundings. At times, I felt like the prince in the story of Rapunzel, trying to liberate her from the locked tower governed by the witch, running the risk of destroying us both, were I to fail. Reis reminds us that whereas the non-psychoanalytic literature regards traumatic repetition as unmeaningful, psychoanalytic approaches to the repetition of traumatic memory have emphasized an opposite approach (Reis, 2009). He focuses on the social aspect of traumatic repetition, asserting that repetition is not addressed to any particular person so much as it is addressed to another. He writes:

The other who can receive this experience is the analyst, who participates not as a blank slate upon which knowledge can be inscribed, but whose affective presence within the relationship with the patient creates the condition for the mutual experiencing of that which exists outside speech. This communication occurs within performative and motoric dimensions of the transference–countertransference, conveying experience that is beyond the limits of human ability to grasp or imagine symbolically (Laub, 1991), yet allows patient and analyst together to create in their encounter an experience of witnessing. . . . the transference acts as the scene of address for the simultaneous repetition and witnessing of traumatic memory in its performative and enactive form. The address does not occur between people, as one might say conventionally, rather it "happens," as an action, within a scene. It is lived, or performed, through what Bollas (2000, p. 112) has described as "a showing by a relocating evocation."

(p. 1365)

I well knew that disclosing traumatic stories of this kind could also have severely negative implications. Davies asserts that

although there are many positive outcomes of disclosure, initially breaking the secret of abuse may engender increased disorganization and symptom exacerbation, such as disturbing flashbacks, reenactments of some aspect of the trauma, or self-punitive behavior evoked by the betrayal of and disloyalty to the family represented by the very act of disclosure, these consequences of disclosure reflect the return of bad objects to whom the adult survivor remains unconsciously and tenaciously attached.

(1994, p. 95)

Davies also relates to the complexity of the process of remembering. She reminds us that "specific traumatic memories are frequently state-dependent" (Van der Kolk, 1989).

They were encoded in trauma-related states of helpless terror and wordless rage and are accessible only when the patient reenters those affective states, sometimes that occurs only when transference and countertransference reaches a level of intensity that triggers evocation of these states. Further complicating the recovery of memories is the fact that traumatic memories were often not encoded semantically but were processed only on a sensorimotor level of cognition. Unsymbolized and unspoken, the abuse remains unorganized and vast within the patient's psyche, where, alive and encased in wordless terror and rage, it works on her from outside her control. To symbolize the experience for the first time, to put words to what happened to her, is eventually to contain the vastness of the abuse, to shrink it from the size and shape of a monstrous bogeyman from childhood to a still painful but more manageable narrative about truly past events.

(Davies, 1994, p. 97)

However, I felt that Miriam's request shrouded some other deep, hidden meanings. The most intimate aspects of this woman's body and soul had been violently and brutally invaded very early in her life. Shadowed by these experiences, she had never created any intimate relationship with either a man or a woman. The only close relationship she had ever known, and which could echo primary experiences of attachment, was one of invasion. In retrospect, I can recall moments in which I thought to myself that if the broadcasting of her most private memories to the general public would indeed serve as an act of breaking and violating her limits, then it would be my way of echoing her primary experiences, my way to come into contact with some non-verbal zones of her psyche, which had, until now, been inaccessible.

Herman addresses this experience of desecration and defilement. She notes that "traumatic events are extraordinary . . . because they overwhelm the ordinary human adaptations to lie . . . generally involve threats to life or bodily integrity . . . they confront human beings with the extremities of helplessness and terror, and evoke the responses of catastrophe" (p. 33). In telling their rape stories, the loss of control and helplessness is often described as the most humiliating part of the trauma. Moreover, as trauma narratives are often fragmented, due to the fact that people with hysteria lose the capacity to integrate the memory of overwhelming life events, helping them to recreate and re-conceptualize their stories has a healing quality. It seems that talking about these events in public, especially in the mass media, has numerous and diverse meanings and implications. The fragile balance between two major dialectic forces – that of breaking the barriers guarding the "safety zone" and violating privacy versus helping to break the silence and thus validating the events – should be carefully maintained. Traumatized persons often perceive themselves as helpless. Suffice to say, it is the therapist's responsibility to guarantee a safe therapeutic setting, which is protected against violation. In contrast, exposing cases and publishing articles – always sensitive issues, in the case of traumatized patients – become absolutely critical. As Herman reminds us:

balance is precisely what the traumatized person lacks. She finds herself caught between the extremes of amnesia or of reliving the trauma, between floods of intense, overwhelming feeling and arid states of no feeling at all, between irritable, impulsive action and complete inhibition of action. The instability produced by these periodic alternations further exacerbates the traumatized person's sense of unpredictability and helplessness.

(1992, p. 47)

Gradually I came to understand that my willingness to bear the dilemma, to carry it long enough and listen to its multiple emerging voices was in itself of curative potential. Any unequivocal and unambiguous ruling, any taking of sides in this dilemma, would be to miss the complexity and multidimensional aspects of my patient's inner world. Miriam invested enormous efforts into safeguarding her world. Her rigid mechanisms helped her to preserve and maintain a sense of cohesiveness, protecting her from disintegration by fortifying her collapsing fortress. However, this behavior also kept her detached, alienated and estranged – no one could get close to her. Despite the extreme distance she kept from other people, she desperately longed for emotional and physical contact. She repeatedly talked about her desire for a close relationship. Over and over again, she talked about how others enjoyed love and intimacy in their lives, while she remained lonely. How could I positively manage this therapy, continue to guard and protect her world, and yet help her establish real close and intimate relationships? How could I share an important and touching experience with her in a compelling manner and, at the same time, continue to respect her limits – both physical and emotional? How could I touch her authentically, without making her feel intruded upon? Struggling with these questions was inevitable in our relationship. My challenge was to keep fighting, and not give up on her.

In retrospect, I now view my ability to simultaneously feel both the need to protect her and the need to disclose her story as a healing experience, so different from her early experience of brutal penetration in which no discussion or mediation was allowed. It is possible that any truly corrective experience requires an accompanying feeling of danger; a risk must be taken. Only in this way can one's sense of self be repaired. A sterile situation – one which is not permeable to danger – may be safe, but not authentic. Such a situation would not necessarily be strong enough to make an actual impression on the psyche or penetrate the primary levels of mental organization, in which early experiences build their stronghold. The real challenge is to establish therapeutic relations which are, on the one hand, safe and protective, thereby providing a corrective experience for the early injuries. On the other hand, the therapist must be able to plumb the deeper levels of mental organization and echo primary experiences. This kind of therapy does not delude the patient into thinking that life is a safe place; any such illusions were broken long ago. In addition, it does not raise false hopes regarding the possibility of never getting hurt again. Rather, this type of therapy calls for creating connections and ways of dealing with what has been experienced as an invasion. It attempts to enable beneficial, healthy disclosure. Such disclosure is only possible if, in the process of publication, an internal discussion also takes place, helping touch upon the multiple meanings of this choice, and made out of free will rather than a repetitive compulsion. This could serve as a new model of exposure, one which also ensures the patient's limits, security and safety.

It is well known that the symptoms of sexually traumatized patients attract attention to an unbelievable secret and, at the same time, push it aside. The dialectic involved in revealing the secret is both an internal and external drama. Perhaps the only way to know something about this drama is in a non-intellectual or ethical way, but to come into emotional contact with my patient, I needed to deal with the dilemma created by her request to talk about her story in public. Her request was an invitation to cope with the challenge of fulfilling the task she had set for me – to raise the awareness of the greater public regarding the phenomena of sexual abuse – by providing a new model that would, at the same time, continue to protect her sense of safety and privacy.

Davies notes that

> it is extremely important that the therapist working with an adult survivor understand that, by dint of his very presence, the original traumatogenic situation is altered. As the therapist bears witness to the reemergence of traumatic memory, as he validates the patient's memories, as they resonate with his own countertransference experiences, as he helps to demystify the sense of unreality that pervades the patient's waking experiences, he permanently alters the survivor's experience that pain, fear and rage can only be safely experienced in isolation.
>
> (1994, p. 214)

Although she could not verbally express it, in her unique way, my patient was "crying out for human contact" even if this desired contact was frightening, or indeed, horrifying. To establish this type of human contact, it was necessary to know more about her world. Indeed, it would be pretentious to think that I could really understand her agony. Therefore, the difficulties that accompanied the writing of this chapter, and dealing with questions regarding whether and how to share her story with others while still protecting her boundaries, represented an important phase in our therapeutic relationship. I hope that the way I finally chose to present the material – without focusing on one particular patient but creating a collage of stories that express only a minuscule part of the common phenomenon of sexual trauma victims living in our society – will be perceived as I intended; as an act of respect.

In one of our sessions, my patient asked me: "So, did you write about my case?" My concrete answer was "Yes, I did, I found a way to do it." However, what was truly meaningful to both of us was not necessarily the writing itself. Rather, the important thing was for me to experience the difficulty related to talking and writing about her story; the challenge of the disclosure and the possibility to feel my own subjective shame and guilt before all these feelings could be translated into words. These experiences not only exemplified the intricate interplay between words and impressions, but they were also my way to subjectively know something about my patient's inner world, some deeper experience that had to precede words, after which I was able to expose part of this knowledge. This was the therapy's way to find words to express countless early experiences and, at the same time, know something about these experiences, which could hardly be expressed by mere words.

References

Bromberg, P. (1991). On Knowing One Patient Inside Out: The Aesthetics of Unconscious Communication, *Psychoanalytic Dialogues*, 1(4): 399–422.

Bromberg, P. (2013). Hidden in Plain Sight: Thoughts on Imagination and the Lived Unconscious, *Psychoanalytic Dialogues*, 23: 1–14.

Davies, J.M. (1994). *Treating the Adult Survivor of Childhood Sexual Abuse*. New York: Basic Books.

Fairbairn, W.R.D. (1943). The Repression and the Return of Bad Objects. In: (1984), *Psychoanalytic Studies of the Personality*. London: Routledge and Kegan Paul, pp. 59–81.

Freud, S. (1896). The Aetiology of Hysteria. In: J. Strachey (Ed. and Trans.) (1962), *The Standard Edition of the Complete Psychological Works of Sigmund Freud, Vol. 4*. London: Hogarth Press.

Gill, M.M. (1982). *Analysis of Transference, Vol.1*. Madison, CT: International Universities Press.

Greenberg, J. (1991). Countertransference and Reality, *Psychoanalytic Dialogues*, 1: 52–73.
Herman, J. L. (1992). *Trauma and Recovery*. New York: Basic Books.
Hoffman, I.Z. (1991). Dissociation: Toward a Social-Constructivist View of the Psychoanalytic Situation, *Psychoanalytic Dialogues*, 1: 47–105.
Khan, M.M. (1969).Vicissitudes of Being, Knowing, and Experiencing in the Therapeutic Situation. In: *The Privacy of Self*, (1974). Madison, CT: International Universities Press, pp. 203–218.
Khan, M.M. (1960). Regression and Integration in the Analytic Setting. In: *The Privacy of Self*, (1974). Madison, CT: International Universities Press, pp. 13–26.
Mitchell, S.A (1988). *Relational Concepts in Psychoanalysis: An Integration*. Cambridge, MA: Harvard University Press.
Reis, B. (2009). Performative and Enactive Features of Psychoanalytic Witnessing: The Transference as the Scene of Address, *The International Journal of Psychoanalysis*, 90: 1359–1372.
Van der Kolk, B. (1987). *Psychological Trauma*. Washington, DC: American Psychiatric Press.
Winnicott, D.W. (1947). Hate in the Countertransference. In: *Through Pediatric to Psychoanalysis*, (1975). New York: Basic Books.

Index

alienation, from self, xi–xii
alpha-function, 64n5
Amir, D., xii, xv, 37–38, 39, 40
Aron, L., 61–62
Austin, J.L., 36
autistic–contiguous position, 15

babies, 2–3, 90–91
Balint, M., 22
behavioral remembering, 29
belles-lettres, xiv–xv, 58, 95–96
Benjamin, J., 61–62, 106, 107–110
Bettelheim, B., 11
Billow, R., 71, 76–77, 79
Bion, W.R., 55, 64n5
Bollas, C., 24–25, 29–30
Borges, J.M., xii, xv
Breuer, J., 6–7
bridge(s): crossing, 29; between languages, psyche, xv, 27; psychoanalysis building, 6; between somatic symptoms, idiomatic expressions, 8, 63; using transitional object for, 14
Bromberg, P.M., 41, 73, 90, 93–94, 97, 111

Carroll, L., 43–44
Cartwright, D., 3–4, 55, 62, 64n5, 91
Castel-Bloom. O., xi
Cermák, F., 75
Civilization and Its Discontents, 49
Cleft Tongue, 37–38
cognitive unconscious, 43
communication: objects as, 70–72; in psychoanalysis, 39–41; semiotic, 40, 101–102, 104, 109–110

compliance, with reality, 86
conservative object, 30
countertransference: addressing, 22; aiding analyst's understanding, 69–70, 73–74; ignoring, 21; in sexual abuse therapy, 114, 118, 121–122; and transference, 77
cutting, 15

Darwin, C., 82–83n1, 96–97
Davies, J.M., 73–74, 94, 112–113, 113–114, 116, 117, 118–119, 120, 121–122, 124
delusional transference, 88
depression, expressed in dreams, 2
domination, 106
dreams: as gateway, 5; and language of psyche, 2: of missing the train, 22–23; objects in, 3–4; in psychoanalytic approaches, 5; truth of, 9; as venue, 25

Ehrenberg, D., 80–81
Eros and Thanatos, 10

Fairbairn, W.R.D., 118
fairy tales: entering therapeutic enterprise, 13; idioms realized in, 11–12; as living fossils, 12, 14; poets using, xii; in psychoanalytic field, 9–10; *see also The Three Feathers*
family environment, 86
fantasy, vs. imagination, 93–94
father: and daughters' individuality, 108–109; Freud on, 106; memories connected with, 54; patient's problems with, 48, 50, 51–52; perception in poetry, 59, 62; sexual abuse by, 112

Freud, S.: as "archaeologist of the mind", 53–54; on childhood sexual abuse, 116; collecting antiquities, 53; on dream language, 27; and folklore, fairy tales, 9, 10; interest in Rome, 48, 49, 50–51; on one-person psychology, 57; Primary Process of, 6; on somatic symptoms, 6–7; topographic model of consciousness, 9; use of symbolic concept, 7–8; on zoology, 49
Freud: A Life for Our Time, 50

Gary, R., 95
Gay, P., 50–51, 53
Gill, M.M., 79
Grossmark, R., 21–22, 78–79, 82

Hate in the Countertransference, 70
Herman, L.H., 115–116, 116, 119, 122–123
Holocaust, 22–23, 24, 27

identification, complementary, 72
idiomatic expressions: aiding understanding of patient, 81–82; both concrete and metaphoric, 16, 27, 96; as bridges, 8, 31–32, 63, 74; concrete realization of, 1–3, 5, 23, 26, 52; connecting to spoken language, xiii–xix; encoded behind behavior, symptoms, 12; identifying and connecting, 55; as part of therapeutic process, 3; realized in fairy tales, 11–12; realizing, 25–33; and somatic sensations, 75
idioms: "backing her up", xiv, 13; "below the surface", xv, 9, 10–11, 57; "bomb(shell)", 60–61; connecting physical, mental actions, 95; Darwin on, 83–83n1; "digging into past", 48, 50, 52, 57; "doesn't smell good", 3, 74, 81; "under the eye", 7; "gnashing of teeth", 82–83n1; "having it all", 6; "heartless", 31; "holding", 14, 16, 22; "lifting one's eyebrow", 83n1; "missing the train", xiii, 23, 25, 26–27, 57, 62–63; "moving", 96; "see red", 83n1; "seeing with own eyes", 8; "slap in the face", 7; "speak their minds", xiv; "stab in the heart", 7; "stand by me", 1; touching primary somatic layers of mind, 55; "turning a blind eye", 83n1; "what's the matter?", 57; "what's the point?", 2
imagination: advancing therapy, 97; creative potential of, 90–91; vs. fantasy, 93–94; in patient–therapist relationship, 41; a physical experience, 42
impression, early, 47
insight, 9
The Interpretation of Dreams, 50
intimate edge, 80

Johnson, M., 42
Jung, C., xii, 26

Kites, 95
Klein, M., 14, 60
Koertner, C., 6–7
Kristeva, J., 39–40, 101, 102, 104–105

Lakoff, G., 42
language: describing embedded experience, 55; enabling symbolization, 14; formed from somatic experience, 16–17; idioms repressed in, 26; as metaphor, 42–43; as performative action, 36–37; playing with, 41; in poetry, 104; pre-verbal, 26, 32; in primary processes, 96; and separation from parent, 38–39, 59; shared between therapist–patient, 40–42, 45; touching deeper layers, 48
language, of psyche: about, xii–xiii; bridge for, xv; contacting, 122; deciphering, 6; difficulty for patients, 36, 37; and dreams, 2–3; of images, senses, 47; verbal vs. primary layers of, 19
lateness, chronic, 19–21
literature, connections in, xiv–xv
Little, M., 70
The Little Prince, 38
living fossil, 12, 14, 54
Loewald, H.W., 27
love, unrequited: and the feminine voice, 101; as inferiority, 102; and lack of recognition, 107; and mourning, 101; of patient, 99, 100

McDougall, J., 8, 31–32
Melancholic Song, 103–105

memory: enactive representational form of, 27; importance of, 27; non-conscious traumatic, 27; traumatic reliving of, 27–28, 121–122
mental organization, symbols in, 26
metaphor, 42, 43, 44
mind, mental life: archaeological layers representing, 52; archaic components in, 54–55; collective unconsciousness in, 26; development of symbolization, 14; idioms touching somatic layers of, 55; preservation in, 49; primary levels of thought in, 32; role of fairy tales in, 9
Mitchell, S.A., 61–62
mother: analyst seeing as, 88; dreams for child, 90–91, 93; phonetic associations with, 38, 57; pre-verbal communication with child, 101; shared experience with, 57; subjectivity studied, 59
mother-tongue, 40
mutual recognition, 59

narcissism, 10
non-verbal language: difficulty of accessing, 35; preserving experience, 26; progressing from, 79; using symbols, images, 6, 57
Not Far from the Center of Town, xi, xv, 17

object relation theory: comparing relationships, 41; patience necessary for, 24; in patient's internal world, 72; and projective identification, 60, 62; on therapist's necessary presence, 86; as traumatic reliving, 28, 30; and two-person psychology, 57; and unrequited love, 101
objective reality, 87
objective subjectivity, 88–89
odor(s): functions, in relationships, 67; hampering therapy, 68–69, 74, 79; patient owning, 76; as potential dangers, 75
Oedipus complex, 10
Ogden, T., 14–16, 60
Other: function of, 63; mutual creation of, 92; as transformative object, 30–31; as witness, 28
outline, of book, xiii–xv

panic phenomenon, 10
Perel, G., 58–59, 61, 63
Petry, S., 39–40
Playing and Reality, 96
poetry: Borges on, xv; challenging linguistic paradigms, 104–105; concrete meaning in, xii; defended as catharsis, 103; expressing linguistic and semiotic modes, 102; feminine, masculine gap in, 104; symbolic, semiotic orders of, 104–105; *see also* Ra'hel
primary experiences: accessing non-verbal areas of, 6; behavioral symptoms associated with, 26; governing behavior, i; idiomatic expressions of, 16; sharing, discussing, 58
primary level, of mind, xiii
Primary Process, 6
"Primitive Emotional Development", 57
projective identification: Bion on, 62; and childhood sexual abuse, 117; communicating feelings, 61; defined, 64n3; used by patients, 60–61
Proust, M., 91
pseudo-language, 37–38
psychoanalysis: aim to enable inner speech, 87–88, 106; on archaic components in mental life, 54–55; commensal, 79–80; development of literature, 58, 59–60, 62; elapsed time in, 24–25; establishing trust, insight, 77–78; imagination, dreaming in, 90–91, 93, 97; internal, external interplay, 100; mental health plus motion, 95; patients depriving oneself, 85–86; patient/therapist relationship, 41; similarities to archaeology, 53–54; using poetic meanings in, 107

Racker, H., 67–68, 72
Ra'hel, 103–105, 110n1; *see also* poetry
Raufman, R., 10, 16, 31
Reality Principle, 92
Reis, B., 22, 27, 29, 33n3, 36, 117–118, 120–121
relational analyst, unobtrusive, 21–22
reverberation, associative, 7
Roberts, R., 100–101
Rome, Freud on, 48, 49, 50–51

Saint-Exupery, A., 38
secondary consciousness, 54
seeing, and understanding, 8–9
self-development, and moods, 29–30
sensory surface, establishing, 15–16
sexual abuse, childhood: difficulties of psychotherapy for, 112–113; disclosing, 113, 119, 121, 122–123; factor in psychopathology, 116; integrating memories of, 120; lifelong pain of, 112; psychology's denial of, 116; public disclosure of, 114–115, 116–120, 122.125; reenactments of, 114; relational model of therapy for, 113–114; repressing, denying, 115–116; secrecy of, 111, 112–113, 119–120, 124
Shakespeare, W., 85
silence, in therapy, 21–22
Slochower, D., 22
smell(s) *see* odors
Smith, A., 102–103, 104–105
social unconsciousness, 24, 26, 32nn1–2, 63
somatic idioms: Darwin on, 83–83n1; defined, 3; lack of discussion on, 8; Ogden ignoring, 16; and verbal idiomatic expression, 16, 75
somatic illness, 31
somatic senses, 2–3
somatic symptoms, 8
speech act therapy, 40
Standing in Front of Me, 58–59, 62, 63
Strangers to Ourselves, 102
Studies on Hysteria, 6–8
supportiveness, 13–14
symbolization, language enabling, 14
Symington, N., 77

Tagore, R., 96
taste, in dream imagery, 3
therapist: as active witness, 28; as analytic object, 89; dealing with patients' sexual abuse, 111–113; disclosing patient's sexual abuse, 120–121; "going mad", 87, 88; in patient's internal world, 95; "presence" of, 62; and projective identification, 60–61; reenacting with patient, 117, 118; and relational psychoanalysis, 61; subjective presence necessary, 86–87; taking on mother's role, 91–93; uniqueness of profession, 63; viewing opposing images of patient, 89–90
therapy *see* psychoanalysis
This Craft of Verse, xii
The Three Feathers, 5, 10–11, 12, 52
Through the Looking Glass, 43–44
Torah, traveling figures in, 100–101
transference: affecting analyst's behavior, 67–68; and countertransference, 16, 77; delusional, 88; in sexual abuse therapy, 114, 118, 121–122
transitional object, 14
Trauma and Recovery, 115–116

understanding, and seeing, 8–9
"Unthought Known", 29, 30–31
Urban Dictionary, 60–61

verbal level, of mind, xiii
von Frantz, M., 9, 10

Winnicott, D.W., 14, 57, 69–70, 86–87, 92, 93, 95–96
witnessing, in therapy, 36, 117–118, 121
women: bending linguistic rules, 103–104; developing feminine self, 109; expressing desire, 107–108; and father's love, 109; feminine voice of, 101–102; subordination in, 106, 108, 109; *see also* sexual abuse, childhood
words, abstract vs. concrete, xii

Yigael, Y., 6, 7, 10, 16, 31

Zoran, R., 103
Zweig, S., 53